P9-CRX-946

KINGFISHER POCKET GUIDE TO

THE NIGHT SKY

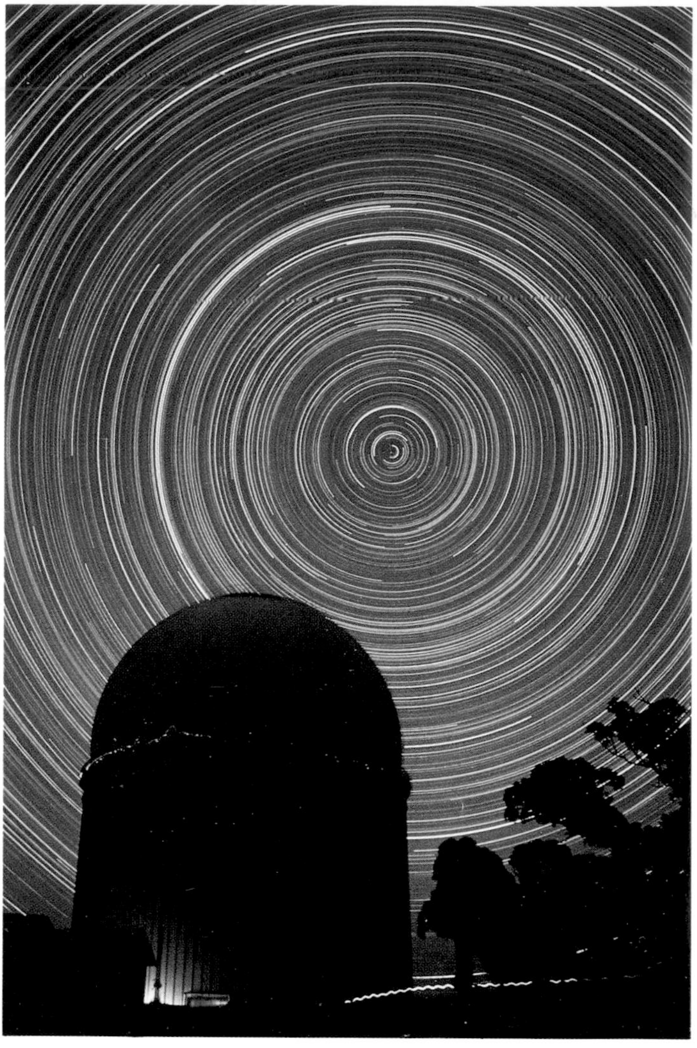

KINGFISHER POCKET GUIDE TO

THE NIGHT SKY

Written by

JAMES MUIRDEN

KINGFISHER
a Houghton Mifflin Company imprint
222 Berkeley Street
Boston, Massachusetts 02116
www.houghtonmifflinbooks.com

10 9 8 7 6 5 4 3 2 1
1TR/1205/WKT/MAR(MAR)/128KMALG/F

First published in this format in 2006

Material in this edition was first published by
Kingfisher Publications Plc in *Astronomy Handbook* 1982

ISBN 0-7534-5996-5
ISBN 978-07534-5996-6

Senior editor: Michèle Byam
Assistant editor: Mandy Cleeve
Coordinating editor: Caitlin Doyle
Designer: Smiljka Suria
Proofreader: Sarah Snavely

Color separations: P+W Graphics, Singapore

Printed in China

Contents

Introduction

Astronomy is a science, but it is also an exciting voyage of discovery. The sky is free for everyone to see—both town dwellers and country dwellers. Everything, from the blinding Sun to the dimmest star, waits to be discovered.

Just like there are different types of objects in the sky, there are also different types of astronomers. Some are referred to as "armchair" astronomers by their more active colleagues since they get their enjoyment from reading and looking at pictures. But true amateur astronomy involves looking at the sky.

► **Some of the stars** in this photograph are more luminous than the Sun, and others are dimmer. They all belong to the Milky Way galaxy—a vast collection of around 500 billion stars. The filmy clouds of gas and dust, or nebulae, will one day form clusters of new stars.

▼ **The 13-foot** Anglo-Australian Telescope (AAT), New South Wales, is one of the "giants."

Amateurs and professionals

Contrary to popular belief, a large majority of amateur astronomers do not have a large telescope. Binoculars are the most common astronomical instrument. Some enthusiasts have observatories in their

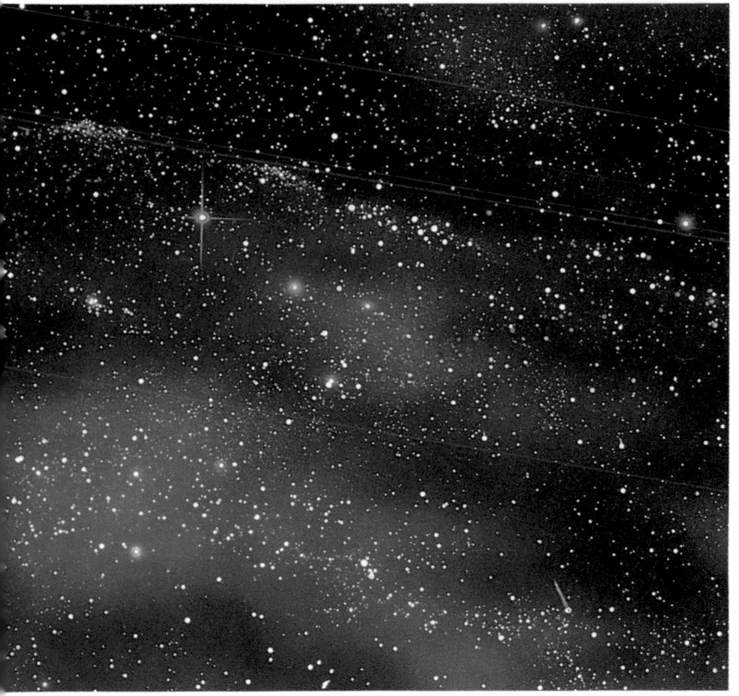

backyards; but it is worth remembering that important discoveries have been made with the naked eye alone. After all, the ancient astronomers—in Greece, China, and Egypt—gathered information with the simplest viewing instruments. Their method was to observe the sky and keep detailed records of everything they saw.

Of course, professional astronomers today have the use of massive telescopes and other sophisticated equipment. For them the sky is literally the limit. Some amateurs become professionals, but then a strange thing happens: they stop gazing upward and spend their time looking at dots on photographs or in the company of unromantic computers. So this book is for true amateurs who want to go out beneath the sky and begin their voyage of astronomical discovery.

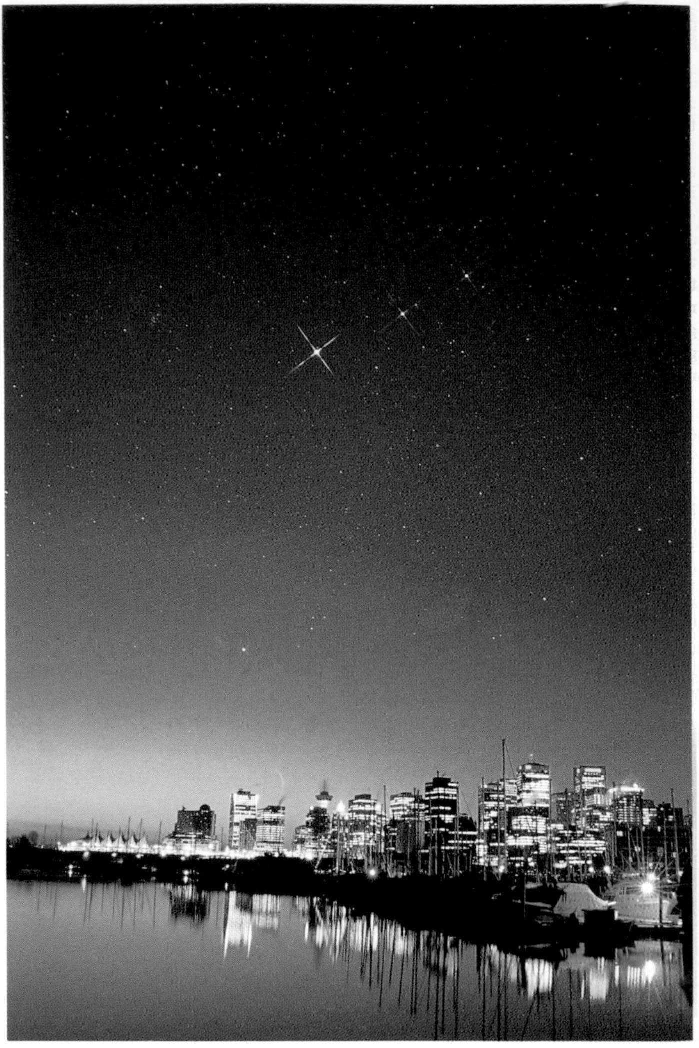

The amateur astronomer

Many amateur astronomers start out as stargazers who regularly scan the night sky, making themselves familiar with the stars and their patterns. Some amateurs become particularly interested in the bodies that make up our solar system: the Sun, Moon, planets, comets, and other smaller objects. Others prefer to look much farther into space, examining the stars, star clusters, and gaseous nebulae that belong to the Milky Way galaxy. They even search for other galaxies—so distant that light takes millions of years on its journey.

◀ **The constellations of Gemini**, the Twins (top) and Orion (right), are familiar winter constellations to amateur astronomers. They are shown here over the city of Vancouver, Canada.

▶ **Comet West**, seen here in 1976, was one of the brightest comets of the 1900s, and some observers even saw the brilliant nucleus in daylight. It was one of the many comets that was discovered by a small group of amateur astronomers who continuously search the night sky for these fleeting visitors.

▼ **The Moon's surface** has been thoroughly surveyed by spacecraft, but amateurs never get tired of gazing at its mountains and craters.

Amateur discoveries

Important discoveries are occasionally made by amateurs, even in today's world of giant telescopes. Some are discovered relatively closeby; others are found in remote regions of space. For example, on Christmas evening 1980 English enthusiast Roy Panther discovered a new comet using a homemade telescope. More recently on February 19, 1992, American amateur Peter Collins was surveying the Milky Way when he noticed a nova—an exploding star—among the thousands of other faint points of light. In Australia Reverend Robert Evans has discovered more than 30 exploding stars in galaxies faraway from our own Milky Way.

Equipment—binoculars

You can enjoy many hours of observation and see thousands of stars without any equipment at all. This is how most amateurs start out. But binoculars and telescopes are useful. They allow you to see more objects in the sky and examine them in greater detail.

Binoculars

Binoculars consist of a pair of identical small telescopes with their light paths "folded" to make them more compact. Although they are not as powerful as a true astronomical telescope, they have the useful advantage of portability and comfortable viewing using both eyes.

An ordinary pair of binoculars will reveal around 30 stars for every single star that can be seen with the naked eye. But they must be held steadily, which means resting them—or your elbows—on a solid support. Otherwise the stars will appear to move around due to your heartbeat and muscular tension.

Binoculars do not provide very high magnification, so they will not reveal planetary details—although good ones will show three or four satellites of Jupiter and the crescent phase of Venus. They will also show the larger craters on the Moon, and through them sunspots can be projected onto a sheet of paper.

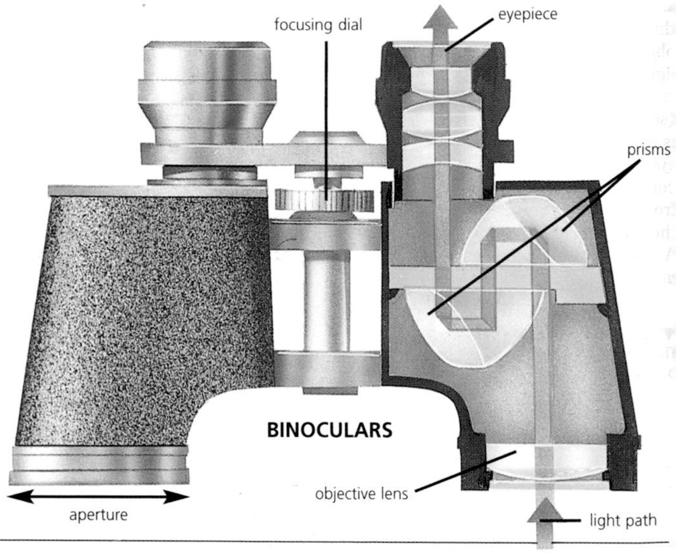

Aperture and magnification

Binoculars and small hand telescopes belong to the same family of low-power instruments. The most important features are the *aperture* and the *magnification*. The aperture is the diameter of the objective lens at the front of the instrument—this is usually between 30–50 millimeters (1–2 in.). The larger this lens, the brighter the image of a star, since more light is being collected.

The magnification indicates how much larger an object looks. The Moon is half a degree across in the sky; through a x 10 telescope it will look five degrees across. The higher the magnification, the smaller the amount of sky that can be seen at any one time.

Binoculars carry labels such as 8 x 30 and 10 x 50. In the first case x 8 is the magnification, and the objective lens is 30 millimeters across; the second has a magnification of x 10 and an aperture of 50 millimeters. For general astronomical work a 10 x 50 instrument is ideal. Higher magnifications are difficult to hold steady.

Refracting telescopes

Some telescopes are refractors: this means that they have an objective lens to collect and focus the light and form an image of the object close to the other end of the tube (see the diagram below). This image is magnified by a small lens called the *eyepiece*. The objective lens should contain two glass components, one in front of the other; if a single lens is used, the image will be colored and blurred. A two-lens objective is said to be *achromatic*, or color-free.

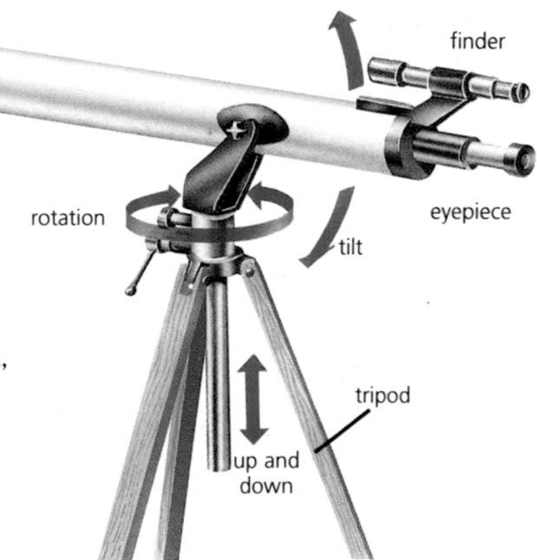

▼ A typical modern refracting telescope. The small finder helps locate objects. The light path through the telescope is shown below.

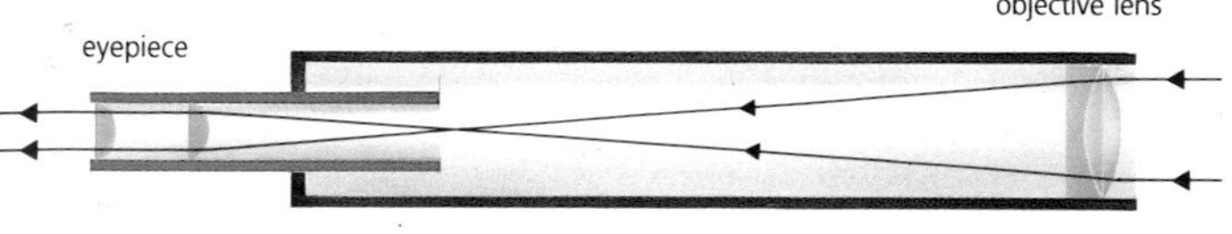

The amateur astronomer

The smallest useful refractor for astronomical purposes has an aperture of 60 millimeters (2.4 in.), but 75 millimeters (3 in.) is much better, and anything larger is really powerful. A refractor's tube is usually around fifteen times as long as the aperture, and this is one disadvantage: refractors are not easy to mount firmly. Many cheap refractors not only give poor definition, but they are mounted on wobbly stands. A poorly-mounted telescope is useless, since no detail can be seen if the image vibrates. Nights when the air is damp and still often give good views. However, dew on optical surfaces can be a problem, and refractors are more affected than reflectors, because the objective lens is so exposed. A cylindrical "dew cap" made of black cardboard, extending around three times the aperture in front of the lens, will help keep the glass bright.

BUYING A TELESCOPE

When you buy a telescope, try to get an experienced observer to look through it before you finally decide. Get in touch with your local astronomical society about this (see page 172); they will be happy to help. A bad telescope could put you off astronomy before you have even started!

Most telescopes are supplied with several eyepieces. To find the magnification, divide the focal length of the eyepiece (this should be marked) into the focal length of the objective lens (the distance from the lens to the image it forms of a distant object). Three magnifications are best, for example:

aperture	magnifications		
60 mm	× 30	× 90	× 150
80 mm	× 40	× 120	× 200
100 mm	× 50	× 150	× 250

Low powers show more of the sky at one time. High powers are needed for fine details.

◀ **The three-foot refractor** at Yerkes Observatory, Wisconsin, is the world's largest. The glass for the huge lens was cast for another projected instrument, which had to be abandoned.

▼ **Two early telescopes**. In front is the long tube of one of Galileo's refractors, made in 1610. It was with this or a similar instrument that he discovered four of Jupiter's moons, Saturn's rings, and the Moon's craters. Behind it is an 18th-century reflecting telescope, with its mirrors arranged so the observer looked "up" the tube as you do with a refractor.

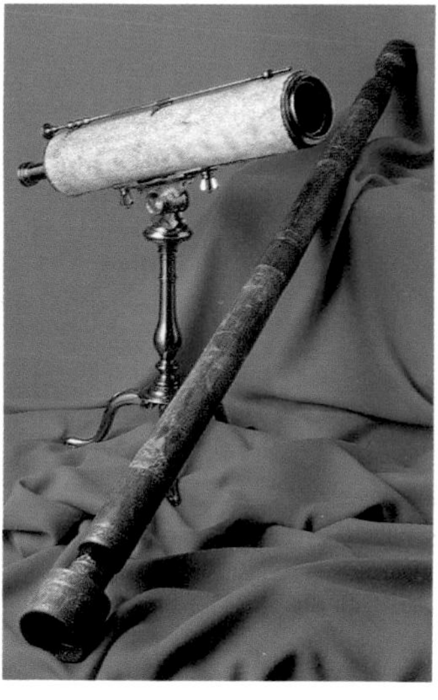

Reflecting telescopes

Reflecting telescopes are only used by astronomers. Their attraction over refractors is that large mirrors are cheaper to produce than lenses of the same size. They are also more compact than refractors, which means that they can be mounted more easily. The smallest commercially-available reflectors have a concave mirror that is around 100 millimeters (4 in.) across. But the best size for an amateur is 150 millimeters (6 in.). A good telescope of this size can give a lifetime of enjoyment.

For good definition the mirrors in a reflecting telescope need to be polished accurately within around one tenth of the wavelength of visible light, or around 0.00005 millimeters of perfection. A Newtonian reflector (see below) consists of a concave mirror of parabolic cross section and a small, flat mirror to reflect the focused light through a hole in the side of the tube. A Cassegrain reflector (also below) has a small convex mirror that sends the light back through the small hole cut in the main mirror.

Other, more complicated, reflectors have been developed, but the Newtonian is the one that most amateurs use. The Cassegrain type is much more expensive. Astronomical mirrors are usually coated with aluminum on the front surface. These coatings must be replaced occasionally, and this is the main drawback of reflectors.

Some amateurs have made reflecting telescopes with apertures of 500 millimeters (20 in.) or more. Because they are so compact, it is possible to mount even very large instruments on simple plywood stands that are easy to transport.

Another popular type of telescope is like a Cassegrain, but it uses a large lens at the front of the tube as well as a pair of mirrors. Known as a "catadioptric" telescope, it has an extremely short tube, which makes it very portable.

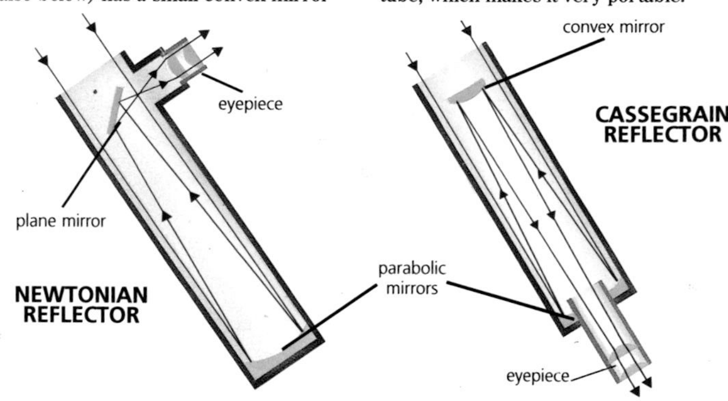

TELESCOPE MOUNTINGS

Telescopes are usually mounted in one of two ways. The simplest is the *altazimuth* mounting. This allows the tube to move vertically and horizontally. To follow a star, you have to swivel the telescope up and around little by little, and this can be awkward.

An *equatorial* mounting avoids this problem, by allowing you to follow the path of a star with just one movement. It has two axes at right angles to each other, like the altazimuth, but one is parallel to Earth's axis. If this (the polar axis) is turned once a day in the opposite direction to the direction in which Earth spins, the telescope keeps pointing in the same direction (see the diagram on the right). The other axis (the declination axis) is only used when you are locating an object to begin with.

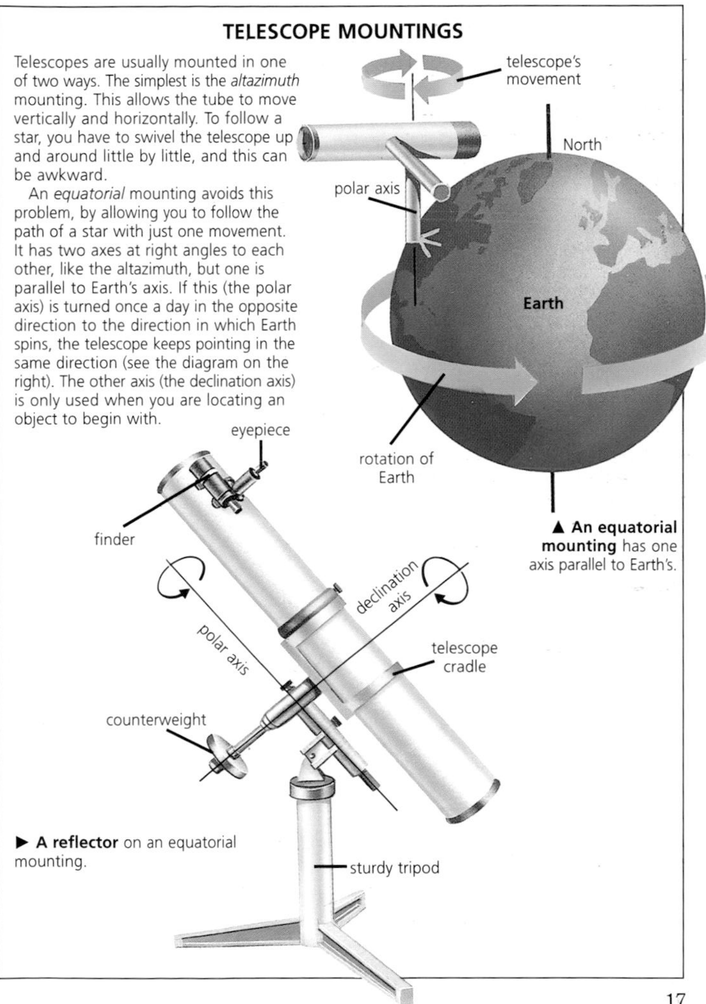

▲ **An equatorial mounting** has one axis parallel to Earth's.

► **A reflector** on an equatorial mounting.

The amateur astronomer

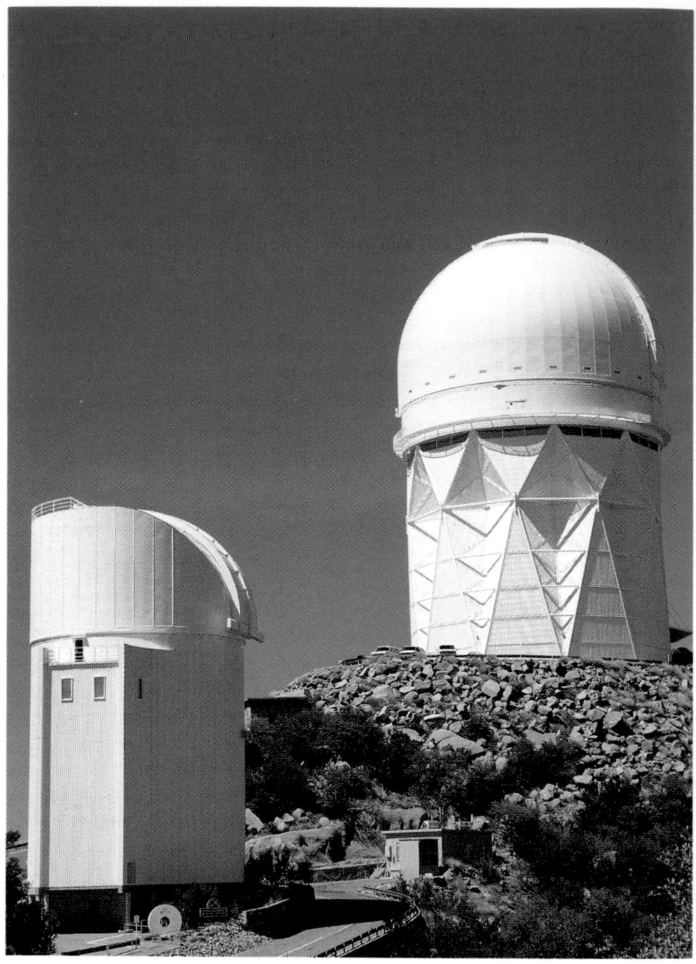

Almost all professional instruments are reflectors; the last big refractor, the three-foot telescope in Yerkes, Wisconsin, was built in 1897.

Many amateurs have built their own reflectors using purchased optics and making the tube and mounting. This is certainly the cheapest way of obtaining a powerful telescope for anyone with a workshop and some skills with tools.

Magnification

The illustration on the right gives you an idea of what an amateur can expect to see. If you hold the book around ten inches (25cm) away, it shows the planets as they can be seen through a telescope magnifying 200 times. Each planet is shown near its maximum and minimum possible distance from Earth (Uranus, Neptune, and Pluto are omitted).

But the telescopic view is never as steady as this; currents in the atmosphere make the image flicker and blur. And a small telescope will reveal less detail than a large one.

A telescope's view

Most astronomical telescopes give an upside-down view. Terrestrial telescopes use extra lenses to give an upright image. Astronomers tend not to use these, because any piece of glass in the light beam makes the image faint.

◀ **The large dome here** houses one of the world's largest telescopes, the 13-foot (4-m) Mayall reflector on Kitt Peak, Arizona. Although telescopes in airless space can obtain much sharper images than those on Earth, there are still many important observing programs that can be done at ground level, and very large telescopes are still being planned.

minimum maximum

MERCURY

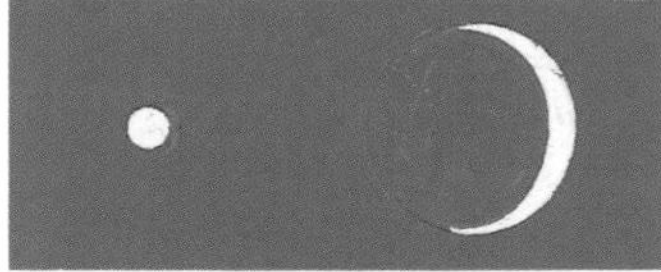

VENUS

MARS

JUPITER

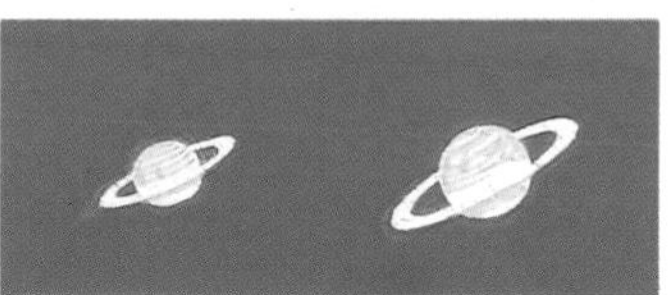

SATURN

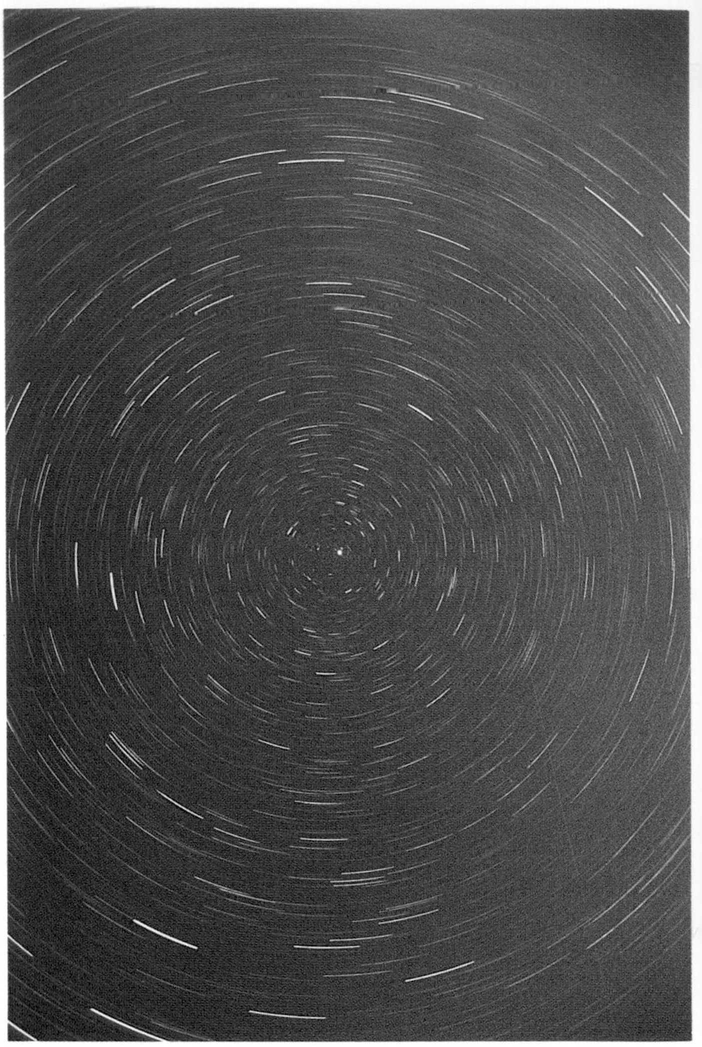

The base from which we observe the sky is moving all the time—but we are so used to living on the spinning Earth that we assume it is stationary and that everything in the universe moves around it. We seem, like the observer in the diagram below, to be in the center of a huge, rotating, invisible sphere—the celestial sphere. The heavenly bodies seem to be attached to the inside of this sphere and carried around it in an east-to-west direction.

Since Earth revolves on its north-south axis, the celestial sphere appears to rotate around the same axis. If a camera is directed toward one of the celestial poles, and the shutter is left open for a few minutes while Earth spins, the stars form trails centered around the pole.

Ptolemy's universe

The illusion that the stars, planets, and Sun revolve around Earth is so convincing that people believed in it for thousands of years. The Greek astronomer Ptolemy (around A.D. 140) figured out a complicated system in which the different planets, the Sun, Moon, and stars all had their own invisible shells or spheres rotating around Earth. These separate spheres were necessary because only the stars keep the same relative positions from night to night. The planets and the Moon move across the sky.

◀ **This 40-minute exposure** shows the sky turning around the Northern celestial pole.

▼ **The celestial sphere.** A celestial object is at its highest when it crosses the meridian.

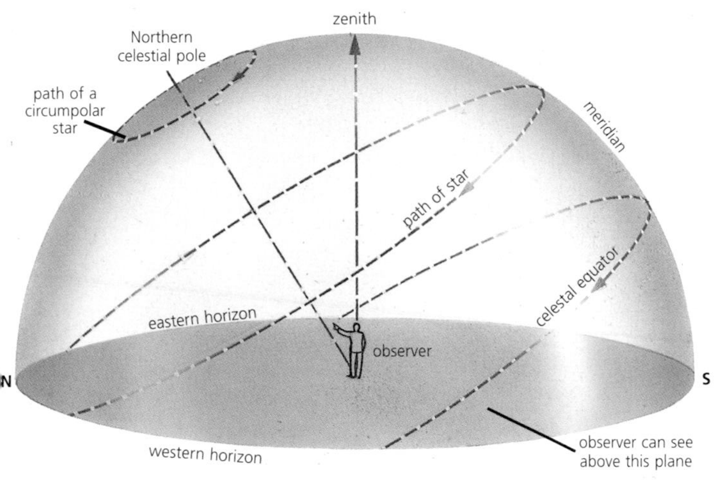

The moving sky

Spinning Earth

Today we know that Earth and everything we see is moving. The stars appear to be in the same place, but they are not stationary. Some are moving very fast, but they are so far away that their position in relation to each other does not seem to change. The planets are closer, and their movement is more noticeable. They revolve around the Sun, and so their positions on the celestial sphere change slowly. The Moon only takes one month to go around the celestial sphere once. The Sun takes one year—the length of time that is taken by Earth to complete one orbit.

▼ **The planets** appear to move around the celestial sphere in an irregular movement, simply because Earth also moves. In Ptolemy's Earth-centered universe these irregularities had to be explained by supposing that each planet moved in a small epicycle, as shown here.

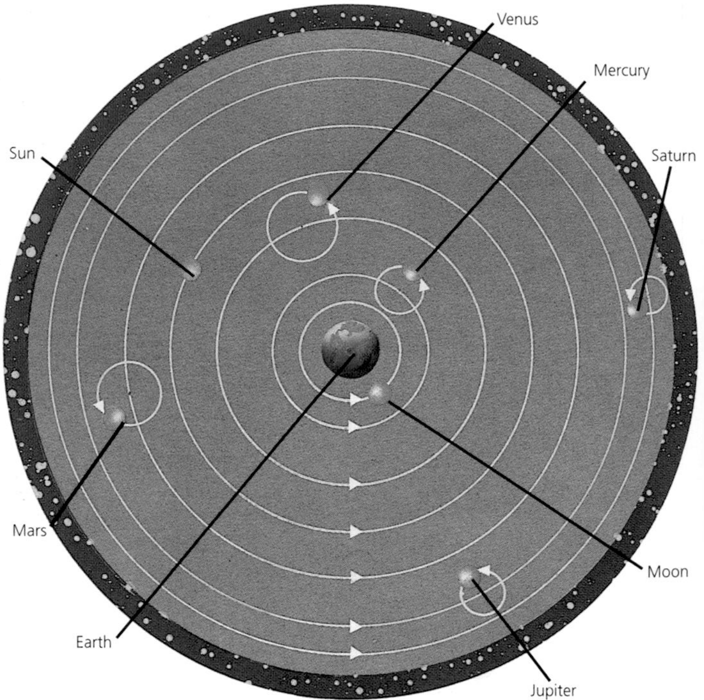

PROVING EARTH'S ROTATION

Jean Foucault's famous experiment to prove that Earth rotates was carried out in Paris, France, in 1851. He hung an iron ball on a wire around 200 feet (61m) long (see above). A heavy weight tends to keep swinging in the same direction while Earth turns underneath it, making the pendulum's direction appear to change.

The longer the thread, the better, and the weight should be as heavy as possible. A good place to hang the thread is at the top of a staircase, but drafts, vibrations, and twists in the thread must be avoided if the pendulum is to keep swinging in the same plane. Mark the path of the pendulum at the start on a simple grid and return later to observe the apparent change of direction.

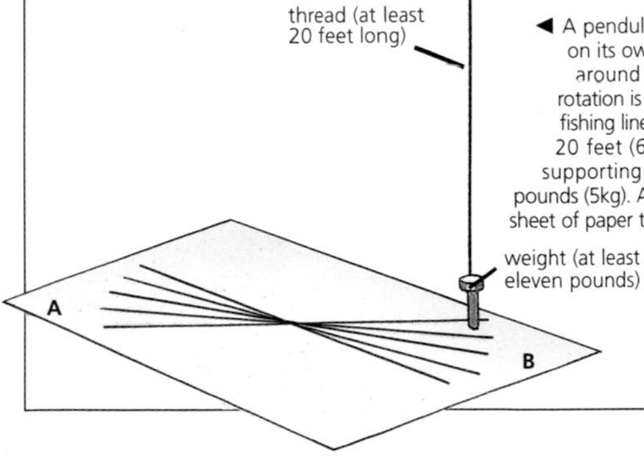

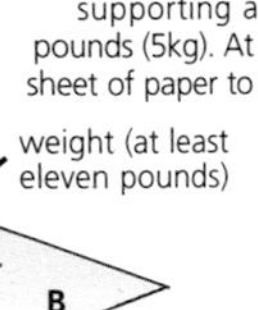

◀ A pendulum needs to keep swinging on its own, protected from drafts, for around half an hour before Earth's rotation is noticeable. The thread (nylon fishing line is suitable) should be at least 20 feet (6m) long and be capable of supporting a weight of at least eleven pounds (5kg). At intervals draw lines AB on a sheet of paper to show its changed direction.

The moving sky

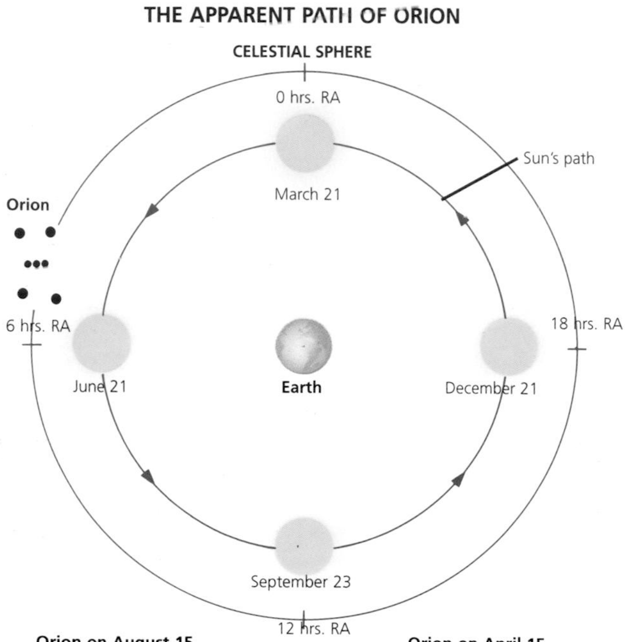

THE APPARENT PATH OF ORION

Orion on August 15

Orion on April 15

Constellations and the seasons

Earth's annual journey around the Sun makes our star appear to travel around the celestial sphere once per year. This affects the visibility of the constellations, since stars cannot be seen in the daytime.

Look, for example, at the diagram on the left. It shows the apparent movement of the Sun as Earth orbits and the famous constellation of Orion. In June the Sun lies in the direction of Orion, which is therefore in the daytime sky and invisible. By August, however, Earth's orbital motion has carried the Sun east of Orion, and it now rises in the morning sky before dawn. By midwinter the Sun appears across from Orion in the sky, and the constellation is in a good location for midnight viewing. By April the Sun has moved in close on its western side, and Orion disappears into the evening twilight once again.

This is the same for almost all the constellations. Because of Earth's movement around the Sun, each one is visible at different times of the year—some only in the winter, and others only in the summer.

THE SEASONS

If Earth's axis was upright, the Sun would pass directly over the equator every day. But the axis is tilted in a fixed direction, 23.5° from the vertical.

On June 21 the North Pole is inclined toward the Sun, bringing midsummer to the northern hemisphere, while the south experiences midwinter. On December 21 the situation is reversed, while the spring and fall occur between these times.

With a clear view of the horizon, record the changing sunrise or sunset point during the year. At the equinoxes the Sun rises exactly in the east and sets exactly in the west.

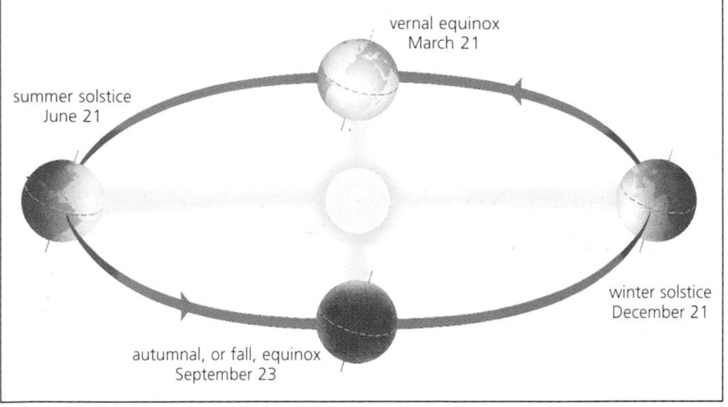

Solar days and sidereal days

Since life on Earth is regulated by day and night, the Sun is used as the basic timekeeper. The normal Sun or *solar* day corresponds to the interval between successive noons or midnights—that is the 24 hour period in which Earth spins once on its axis.

But as Earth orbits the Sun at the same time as it spins, the solar day does not indicate the true rotation of Earth in space with respect to the stars.

Look at the diagram on the right. On day 1 it is noon to one observer and midnight to the other. One *sidereal* day later (day 2) it is not quite noon and midnight again, since Earth has moved a little distance along its orbit and must spin slightly more to bring the Sun back to where it was.

Since most astronomers observe the Moon, planets, and stars, their telescopes are adjusted to turn on their polar axis in one sidereal day (23 hrs. 56 mins.), the time the celestial sphere takes to rotate once. The amateur must remember that each month the constellations will be in the same positions two hours earlier and that every night the stars appear to rise four minutes earlier. On page 65 you will see how sidereal time indicates which constellations are good for observation.

The position of a city or river on Earth can be found on a map using latitude and longitude. The position of an object on the celestial sphere is also described in these terms, but latitude is called *declination*, or *dec*, and longitude is *right ascension*, or *RA*. These are the celestial or astronomical coordinates.

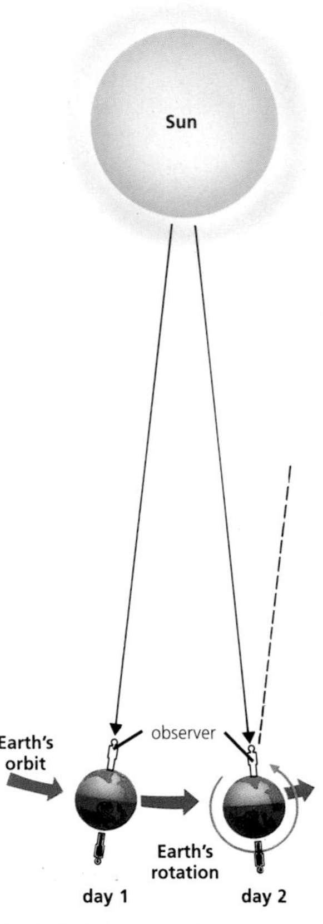

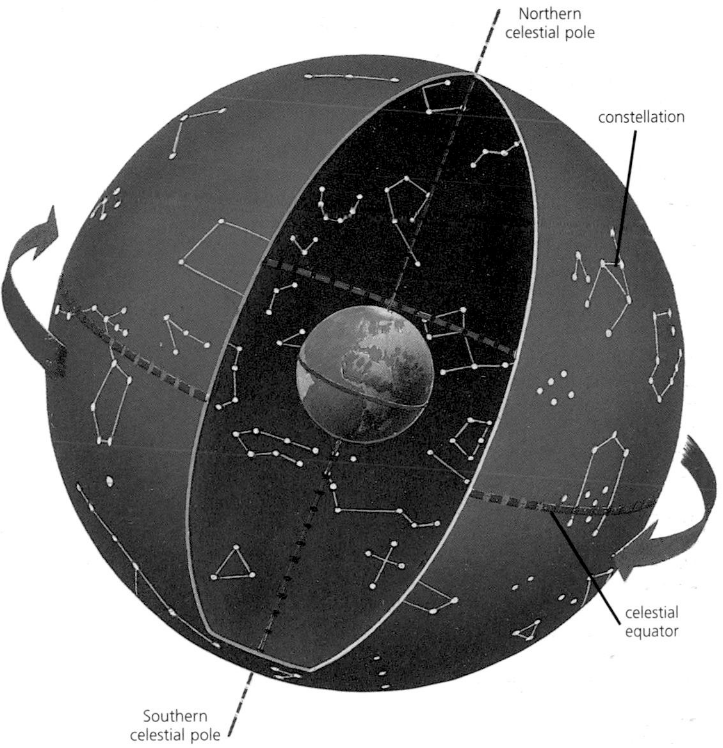

CELESTIAL COORDINATES

Declination is determined in degrees north (positive) or south (negative) of the celestial equator—the line dividing the celestial sphere into two halves, in the plane of Earth's equator.

Right ascension is divided into 24 sidereal hours, measured eastward from 0 hrs., which is the RA of the Sun on the first day of the northern spring (March 21).

The sidereal time is equal to the RA that is due south (or due north to a southern observer) at any instant and is shown by special astronomical clocks.

Constellations and the Sun

The celestial equator and poles are useful for defining the grid of celestial latitude and longitude, but they are not of any "astronomical" importance. They simply correspond to the way our insignificant Earth spins. The significant plane is the *ecliptic*.

The ecliptic is the plane of Earth's orbit. If the Sun was dimmer than the full Moon—so that the stars could be seen during the day—the ecliptic could be plotted on the celestial sphere by noting the Sun's position in front of the stars during the course of one whole year. (An equally good method, if it was possible, would be to stand on the Sun and observe the annual course of Earth in front of the stars.) Once it is plotted in this way, it is found that the plane of the ecliptic crosses the plane of the equator at an angle of 23.5°.

The orbital planes of the Moon and planets coincide relatively closely with that of Earth. They are always to be found within a few degrees of the ecliptic, in a band known as the *zodiac*. The word means "circle of animals" and refers to the constellations: Aries, Taurus, Gemini, Leo, Cancer, Virgo, Libra, Scorpius, Sagittarius, Capricorn, Aquarius, and Pisces. These star groups make up the sequence of

▼ **This map shows** the Sun's path or ecliptic around the celestial sphere. Its position on the first day of each month is indicated by a yellow circle. The planets are always to be found within the 18° band, the zodiac, centered on the ecliptic.

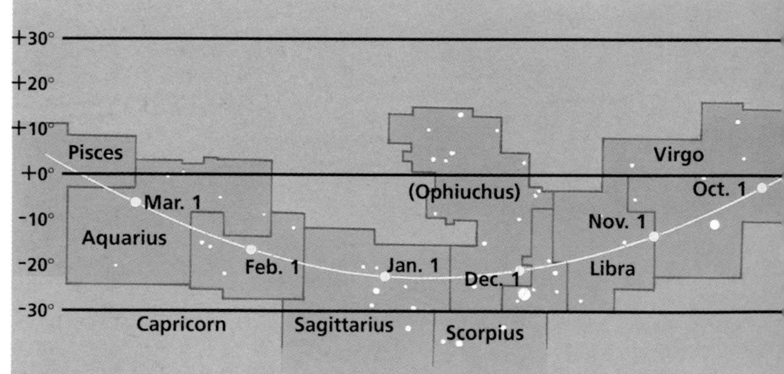

constellations through which the Sun, Moon, and planets all pass. At the beginning of the summer in the northern hemisphere the Sun lies on the borders of Taurus and Gemini. At the beginning of the winter it lies in the constellation of Sagittarius. It crosses the celestial equator in the constellations of Pisces (at the beginning of spring) and in Virgo (at the beginning of fall). In the southern hemisphere these positionsrepresent the opposite seasons.

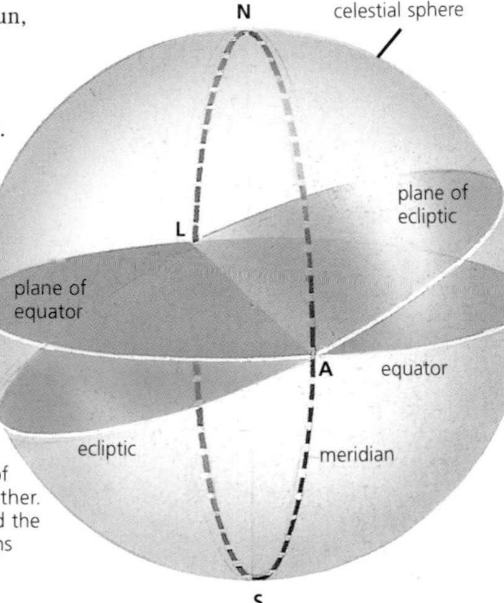

▶ **This diagram** shows how the planes of the equator and the ecliptic cross each other. The points marked "L" and "A" are called the equinoxes. The Sun occupies these positions at the beginning of the northern fall and spring respectively.

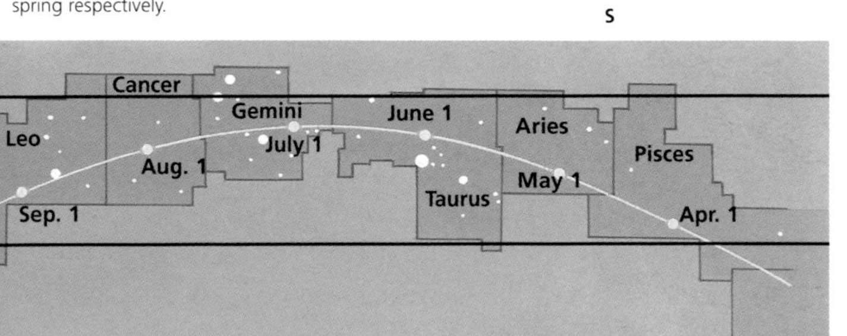

The Sun—our star

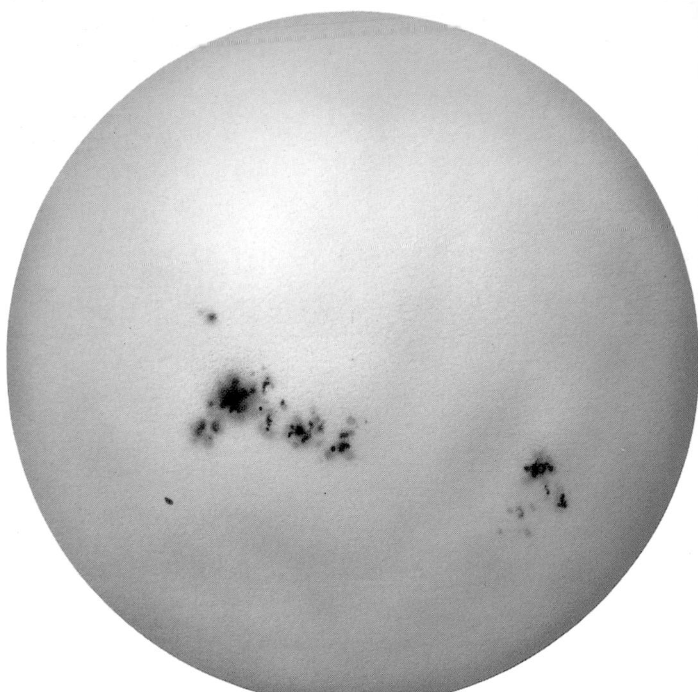

There is nothing strange about the Sun, apart from its proximity. It is around one quarter of a million times closer to us than the next known star, which means that we can examine it in much more detail than any of its neighbors. Solar astronomy is a particularly important subject, and amateur observers can enjoy studying the Sun's surface, as long as they take adequate precautions (see pages 36–37).

Remember that you must never look directly at the Sun.

Long before serious astronomy began, the Sun's daily motion across the sky and annual movement around the celestial sphere were studied. Farmers, for example, would use the Sun's position to tell them when they should plant crops. As was shown on page 25, the seasons are caused by Earth being tilted on its axis. This also affects the position of the Sun throughout

SUN FACTS

diameter: 863,040 miles (109 × Earth)
mass: 328,000 × Earth
volume: 1,300,000 × Earth
surface temperature: 9,932°F
core temperature: around 27,000,032°F
true equatorial rotation period: 25.38 days
apparent equatorial rotation period: 27.28 days
mean distance from Earth: 92,752,000 miles
cosmic year (time to orbit our galaxy): 225 million years
estimated age: 4.6 billion years

the year. In the winter it never rises as high in the sky as it does in the summer, and the points on the horizon at which it rises and sets shift with the seasons.

This changing position of sunrises and sunsets throughout the year gave early civilizations the basis of a calendar. They must have realized that these positions repeated themselves, so that natural or artifical markers could be used to decide the time when different seasons began. Stonehenge, in England, is the most famous structure to determine the moment of the midsummer sunrise.

▼ **The Sun's daily path** across the sky changes with the seasons of the year.

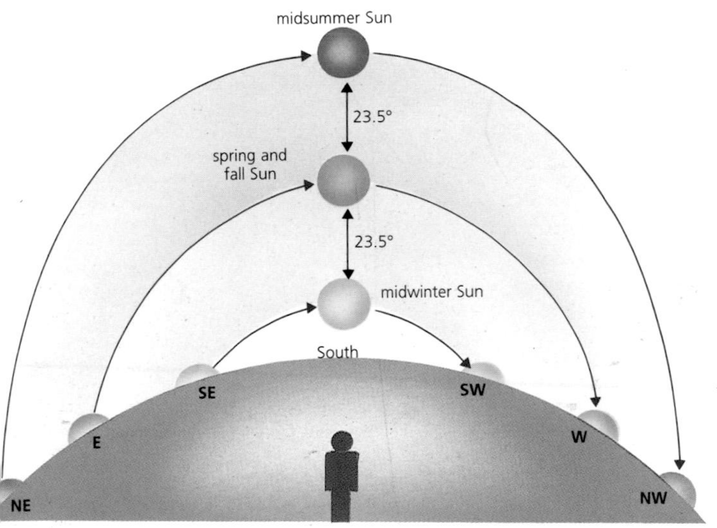

Time and the Sun

The shadow that is cast by a sundial indicates the approximate time of day. It is rarely exactly right, because the Sun moves several degrees east and west of its "true" position.

This happens mostly because Earth's orbit is slightly elliptical, and its orbital velocity varies, making the Sun appear to move quickly or slowly. Clocks are therefore regulated to mean solar time, known as Greenwich mean time (GMT) or Universal time (UT). The difference between this and sundial time (or apparent solar time) is known as the *equation of time* (see right).

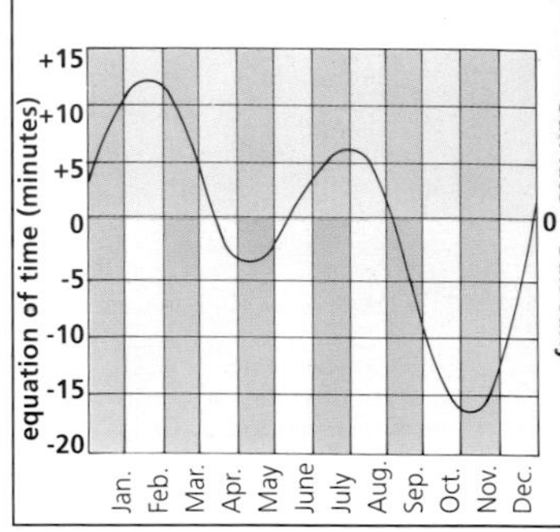

Simple sundials

The simplest sundials consists of an upright stick in the ground. When the shadow points exactly north (or south in the southern hemisphere), it is apparent noon. The equation of time correction will give true noon, but this will only agree with mean solar time if the sundial is exactly on one of the world's standard meridians.

In the summer the shadow cast by the stick is shorter than it is in the winter. If the position of the shadow's tip is marked at true noon every few days throughout the year, the *analemma*, the shape shown below, will be produced. Use this graph to deduce true local time from a sundial. In the green area add the equation of time to the dial's shadow reading; in the yellow area, subtract it.

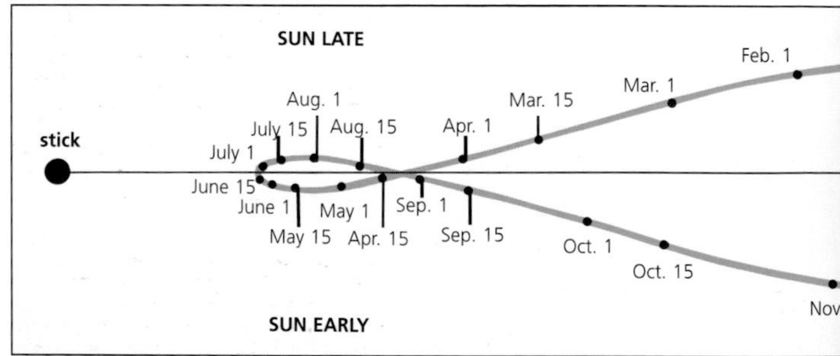

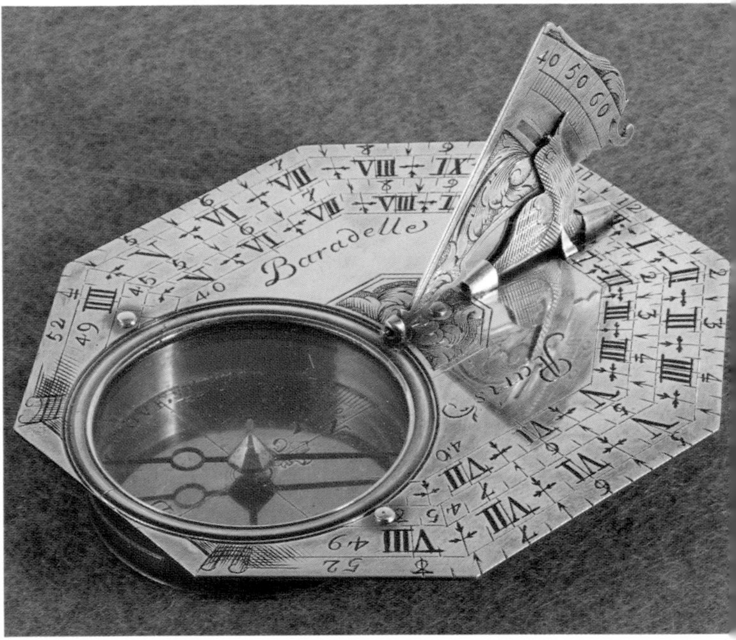

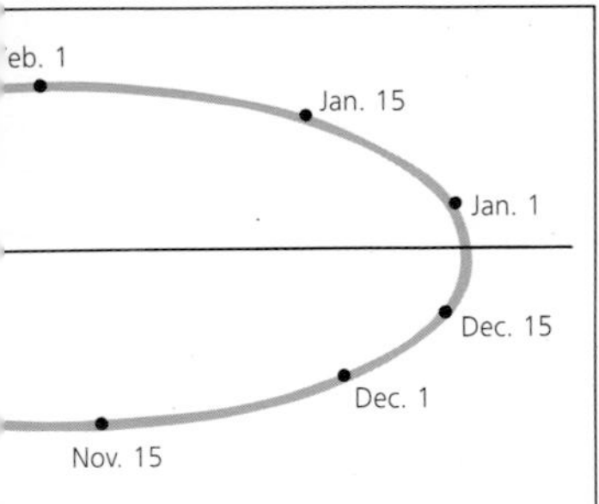

▲ **A sundial's gnomon**, which casts the shadow, has to be parallel with Earth's axis. This means that its altitude is equal to the latitude, and it is aligned north-south. In the portable sundial seen here a magnetic compass and level are used to adjust it before a reading is taken. The altitude of the gnomon is adjustable for use in different latitudes, and the time is read off the horizontal plate.

◀ **A shape like that on the left** is known as the analemma. This is the locus of the tip of the midday shadow cast by a stick throughout the year. The higher the latitude on Earth's surface, the more elongated the analemma becomes.

Sunspots and the solar cycle

The Sun has shone steadily for billions of years, but its surface, the *photosphere*, does not always look the same. Dark spots come and go, and the number that are visible follows a cycle of around eleven years. This cycle also affects the shape of the Sun's faint atmosphere, or *corona*, which can only be seen during a total eclipse.

A sunspot is caused by a very strong magnetic field that is generated from the swirling material beneath the photosphere. Radiation from the interior is sucked away, leaving a cooler, darker area above. Sunspot interiors are around 1,000°F cooler than the photosphere, but they are still hotter than the surfaces of many stars and only appear dark by contrast.

If the image of a dark sunspot is projected onto a screen, it is seen to consist of a dark center, the *umbra*, and a lighter surrounding area, the *penumbra*. Many spots occur in pairs, and a large group lasts for several weeks, or even months, and may be ten times Earth's diameter in its extent. At its maximum activity a dozen different groups may be visible at the same time and, as the Sun rotates, new sunspots come into view.

▼ **Sunspot groups**, such as these, are several times larger than Earth. Their frequency rises and falls every eleven years, but even at their "minimum" activity there are usually some small spots that are visible.

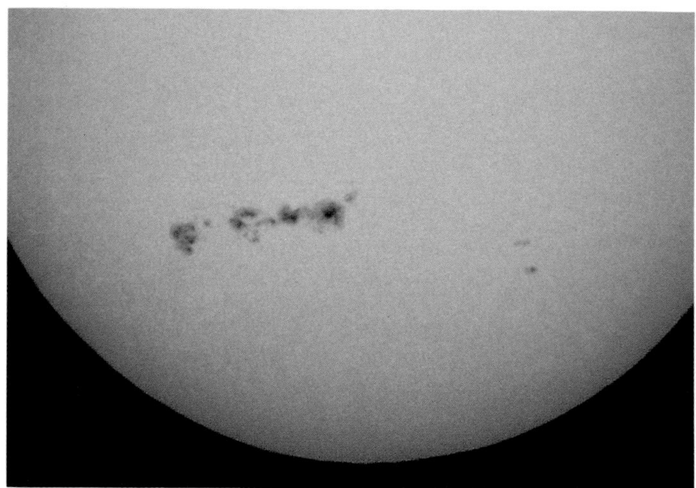

▼ **These drawings** of the Sun were made by projecting its image with binoculars at an interval of two days. The dotted line represents its equator.

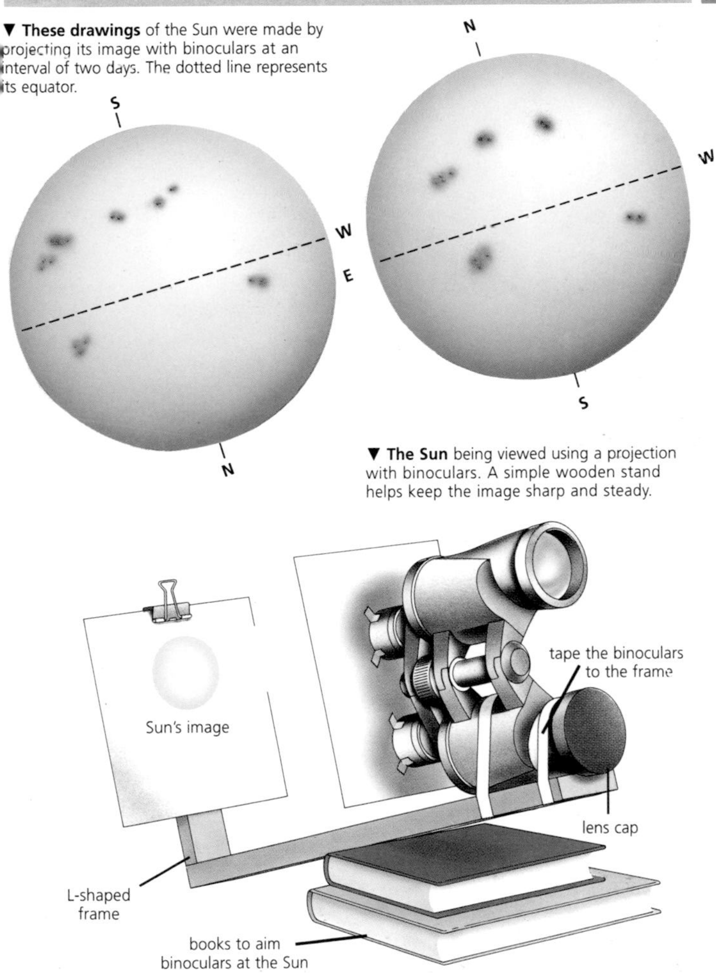

▼ **The Sun** being viewed using a projection with binoculars. A simple wooden stand helps keep the image sharp and steady.

The Sun—our star

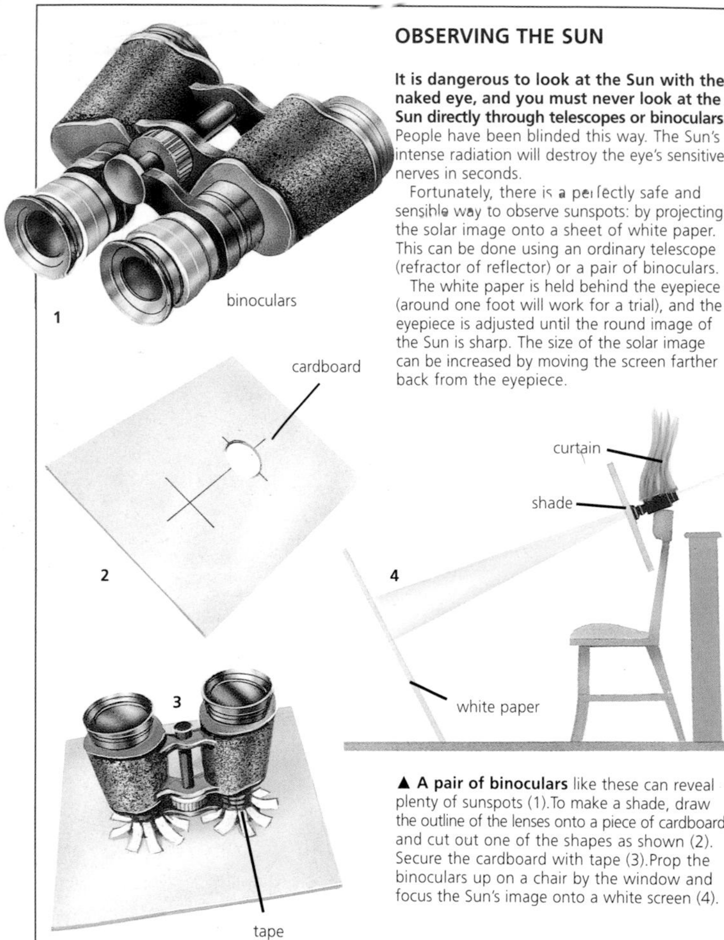

OBSERVING THE SUN

It is dangerous to look at the Sun with the naked eye, and you must never look at the Sun directly through telescopes or binoculars. People have been blinded this way. The Sun's intense radiation will destroy the eye's sensitive nerves in seconds.

Fortunately, there is a perfectly safe and sensible way to observe sunspots: by projecting the solar image onto a sheet of white paper. This can be done using an ordinary telescope (refractor of reflector) or a pair of binoculars.

The white paper is held behind the eyepiece (around one foot will work for a trial), and the eyepiece is adjusted until the round image of the Sun is sharp. The size of the solar image can be increased by moving the screen farther back from the eyepiece.

▲ **A pair of binoculars** like these can reveal plenty of sunspots (1).To make a shade, draw the outline of the lenses onto a piece of cardboard and cut out one of the shapes as shown (2). Secure the cardboard with tape (3).Prop the binoculars up on a chair by the window and focus the Sun's image onto a white screen (4).

The image must be screened from direct light, or its details will be washed out. A projection box (right), with a hole cut in the side to reveal the image, gives a very bright view. But even a simple shade will be adequate. A viewing box is especially useful if a highly-magnified image is being projected, because it improves the contrast of the much fainter image.

It is fascinating to watch a sunspot group develop from day to day: keep an eye on the Sun's eastern limb, because this is where its rotation will bring new groups into view. You can keep a useful record of solar activity simply by counting the number of groups that are visible every day.

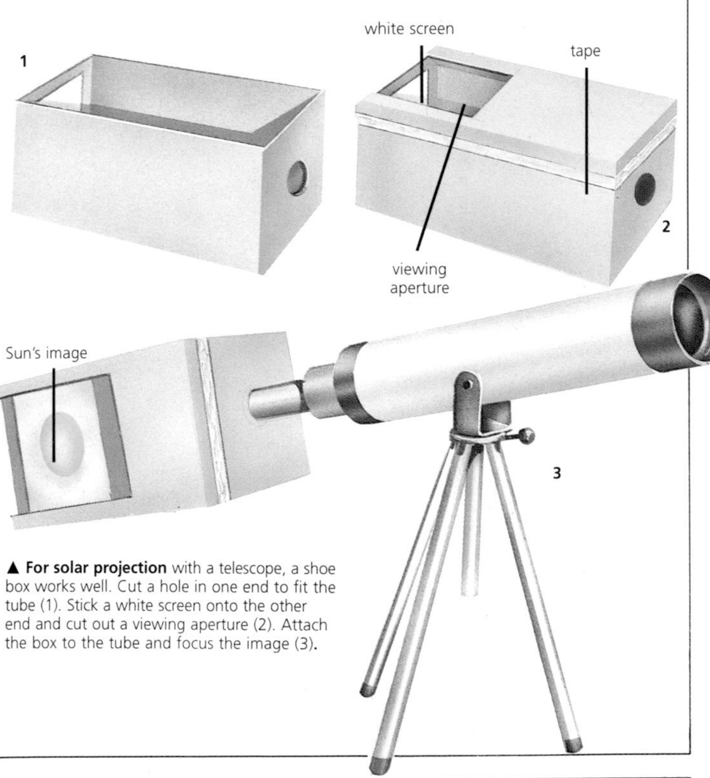

▲ **For solar projection** with a telescope, a shoe box works well. Cut a hole in one end to fit the tube (1). Stick a white screen onto the other end and cut out a viewing aperture (2). Attach the box to the tube and focus the image (3).

The Sun—our star

Observation notes

Observing sunspots is—or should be—a daily business. The simplest method is to count the groups that are visible. After each month add up the total number of groups that you have observed and divide this by the number of days on which the observations were made. The result is the Mean Daily Frequency (M.D.F.) for the month.

Another interesting project is to draw the solar disk with its spots. The easiest way is to make a projection grid (below) and focus the Sun's image onto it. Make a note of the positions of the spots on the grid. Then copy them onto a thin sheet of paper, showing the Sun's circular outline, laid over an identical grid so that the lines show through.

However, before you start you must fix the cardinal points on the disk. Leave the telescope fixed and let the Sun's image drift across the screen. Twist the grid so that the sunspot trails accurately along the east-west line, and you know that the image is oriented correctly. Most astronomical telescopes give an inverted view.

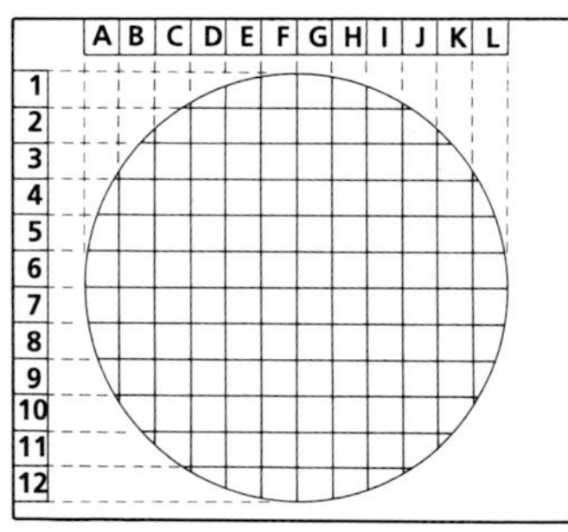

▼ **It is not always easy** to tell which way is north, south, east, or west on the Sun! These two pictures show the orientation of the projected image using binoculars (top) and an inverting astronomical telescope (below). Observers in the southern hemisphere should reverse these directions. It helps to remember that the Sun drifts toward the west.

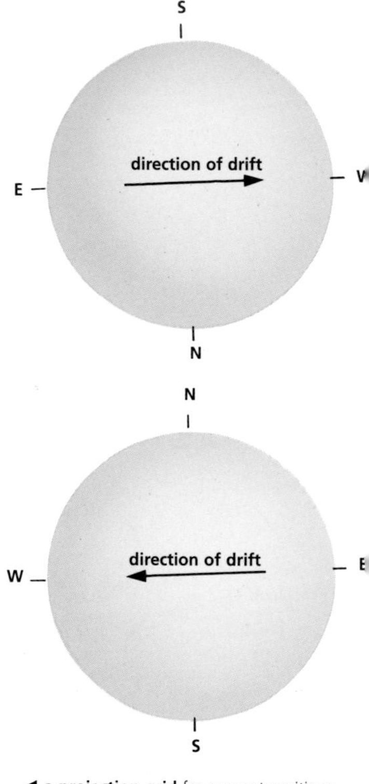

◀ **a projection grid** for sunspot positions.

Solar eclipses

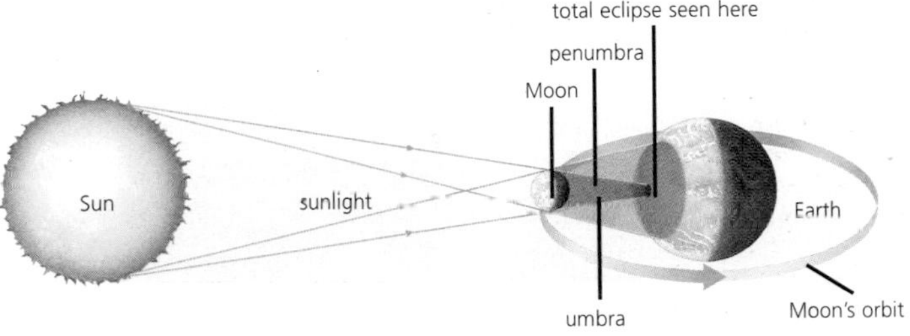

By coincidence the Sun and Moon appear to be around the same size in the sky. When the Moon passes in front of the Sun, it can completely block out the solar disk. Darkness falls, and the faint outer atmosphere, or corona, shines out around the black lunar outline during the seconds or minutes that the total eclipse lasts (see photograph on right).

To see a total eclipse, you must be within the Moon's shadow as it sweeps over Earth's surface, and this shadow is rarely more than a couple hundred miles wide. Outside the central shadow, or umbra, is the wide penumbra, in which only a partial eclipse is seen.

In addition to the pale corona, the red prominences—colossal eruptions of hot gas many times the size of Earth—can often be seen shining around the edge of the Moon. Such a sight is definitely worth a long journey to see!

TOTAL SOLAR ECLIPSE TABLE

date	maximum duration	area of visibility
2006 Mar. 29	4 mins. 7 secs.	Africa, Europe, west Asia
2008 Aug. 1	2 mins. 27 secs.	Canada, Europe, Asia
2009 July 22	6 mins. 39 secs.	India, China, Pacific, Hawaii
2010 July 11	5 mins. 20 secs.	southern South America, south Pacific
2012 Nov. 13	4 mins. 2 secs.	Australia, New Zealand, south Pacific
2015 Mar. 20	2 mins. 47 secs.	Iceland, Europe

The stars

When the stars shine on a clear night, the sight is both confusing and incredible. Any attempt to organize them into constellations appears hopeless. The only definite first impression you may have is that some stars are very bright and others can only be glimpsed.

In fact, this simple observation raises an important issue. Imagine that the stars have the same true brightness, or luminosity. Then the faint ones must be farther away than the bright ones, just as a nearby streetlight outshines one farther down the road. But if instead you imagine that the stars are equally distant, then the bright-looking ones must be more luminous than the faint ones.

The early astronomers, who believed that the stars were attached to an invisible sphere, clearly held the second opinion. But one of the first men to study the stars seriously, William Herschel (who discovered the planet Uranus in 1781), worked on the assumption that the stars are all equally luminous and tried to gauge their relative distances by measuring their brightness in the sky.

Neither one of these simple theories is correct. Some stars are more than one million times more luminous than others, while the closest ones are thousands of times nearer than the most remote stars that have been detected in our galaxy. But luminous stars are more conspicuous, simply because they can be seen at farther distances.

▶ **The Veil Nebula** in Cygnus—an enormous "bubble" of material from an ancient star explosion. It now measures around five times the Moon's diameter in the sky.

Brightness and magnitude

The brightness of a star is measured in *magnitudes*. One magnitude step means a brightness ratio of 2·512. This number is chosen so that a 5-magnitude difference corresponds to a brightness ratio of exactly 100. In other words, a 6th magnitude star

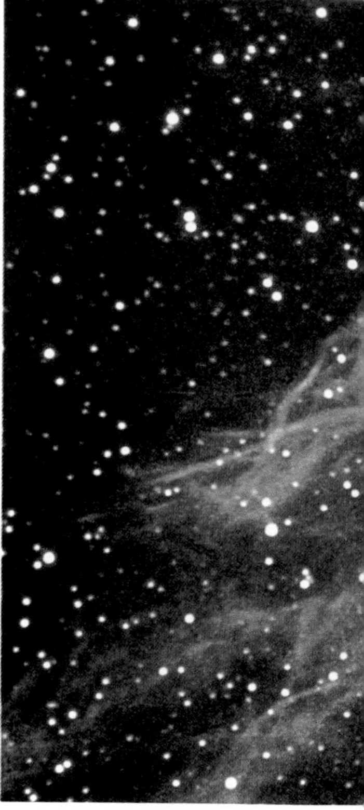

is exactly 100 times fainter than a 1st magnitude star. The larger the number, the fainter the star. Stars that are brighter than magnitude 0 stars are given a negative magnitude.

Apparent magnitude indicates a star's brightness in the sky. The original apparent magnitude scale was developed by the astronomer Hipparchos in 130 B.C., who called the faintest naked-eye stars magnitude 6 (often written mag 6) and the brightest stars magnitude 1. His rough estimates were refined when light-measuring methods were developed, and

the scale was extended from zero into negative numbers. The brightest star in the sky, Sirius, has an apparent magnitude of −1·47. The faintest stars that are detectable with a 150-millimeter telescope are around magnitude 13, or more than 600,000 times fainter than Sirius.

Observing in Mediterranean skies, the 6th magnitude stars of Hipparchos are much dimmer than the faintest stars visible to modern observers living in cities and urban areas, who may not be able to see anything dimmer than the 3rd magnitude. The principal cause is not dust and dirt, which is much less than it was in the coal-burning age, but "light pollution"—artificial light directed up into the air. This brightens the night sky by illuminating hydrocarbons from vehicle exhausts and industrial waste.

Absolute magnitude indicates a star's luminosity; it is the apparent magnitude it would have if it was viewed from a distance of 32.6 light-years. (A light-year, l.y., is the distance that light travels in a year: around 5,890,000 miles.) The most luminous known stars are around magnitude -7. The Sun's absolute magnitude is 4·8—around 40,000 times fainter. However, some nearby stars of around one millionth of the Sun's luminosity have been detected, so the Sun lies in the upper half of the brightness table.

▼ **The patterns** that the stars make in the sky do not reveal their distribution in space. The stars forming the constellation of Orion appear to be projected on the celestial sphere in the pattern shown below left. In fact, they are at very different distances from the Sun, as shown in the illustration below right. (Imagine that the Sun is located below the illustration.)

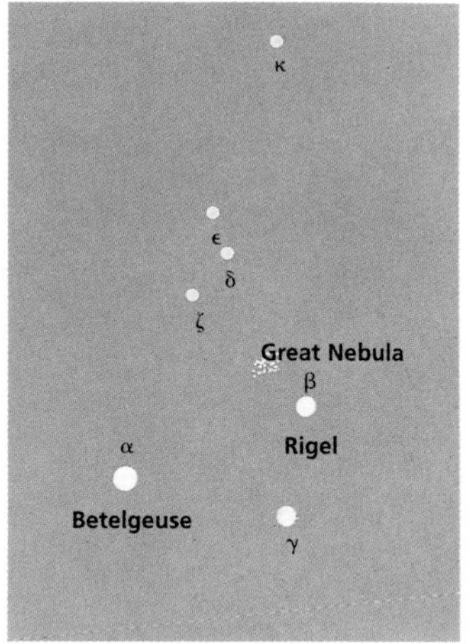

THE BRIGHTEST STARS IN THE SKY

star	constellation	magnitude app.	magnitude abs.	type	distance (l.y.)
Sirius (α)	Canis Major	-1·47	-1·4	dwarf	8.7
Canopus (α)	Carina	-0·7	-8·5	supergiant	1,200
Rigil Kent. (α)	Centaurus	-0·3	-4·4	dwarf	910
Arcturus (α)	Boötes	-0·1	-0·3	giant	36
Vega (α)	Lyra	-0·0	-0·6	dwarf	26
Rigel (β)	Auriga	-0·1	-0·3	giant	45
Capella (α)	Canis Minor	-0·3	-2·6	subgiant	11
Procyon (α)	Eridanus	-0·5	-1·6	subgiant	85
Achernar (α)	Centaurus	-0·6	-5·1	giant	460
Hadar (β)					
Altair (α)	Aquila	-0·8	-2·2	giant	16
Acrux (α)	Crux	-0·8	-3·9	subgiant	360
Betelgeuse (α)	Orion (var.)	-0·8	-5·5	supergiant	310
Aldebaran (α)	Taurus	-0·9	-0·3	giant	65
Spica (α)	Virgo	-1·0	-3·5	dwarf	260
Antares (α)	Scorpius (var.)	-1·1	-4·5	supergiant	330
Pollux (β)	Gemini	-1·15	-0·2	giant	35
Fomalhaut (α)	Piscis Austrinus	-1·2	-2·0	dwarf	420
Mimosa (β)	Crux	-1·2	-5·0	giant	570
Deneb (α)	Cygnus	-1·3	-7·5	supergiant	1,800

STAR SIZES

Stars vary greatly in size. Dying white dwarf stars (page 47) are too small to be shown here. The Sun is much smaller than giant and supergiant stars, like Antares and Betelgeuse, but these are huge because they have been puffed up by internal pressure. Their average density is around one thousandth of the air that we breathe.

It is important to remember that star masses (the amount of material in them) do not vary by nearly as much as their diameters do. Even a large star like Betelgeuse, whose volume is millions of times greater than the Sun's, only has around twenty times its mass.

Stars appear as pinpoints in any telescope, but in the case of the closer and larger stars it is possible to "process" their light and figure out how large they must be. Betelgeuse has an average diameter that is greater than the orbits of Mars, Mercury, Venus, and Earth. It was first measured in 1920.

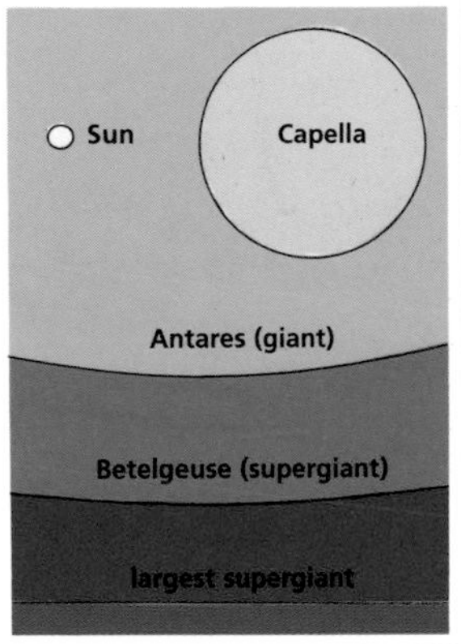

Known as *proper motion*, this movement of the stars is the clue to their likely neighbors. However, even the largest proper motion amounts to a shift that is equal to the Moon's width in 180 years, and most are a tiny fraction of this.

Distances in the sky

Distances between the stars are so great that remote Pluto only seems a step away. If the Sun is represented by a ping-pong ball, Pluto is a speck of dust around 492 feet (150m) away, while the closest star will be another ball around 620 miles (1,000km) away. The compactness of the solar system is difficult to visualize.

The brightness of a star is not a sure guide to distance, since star luminosities vary so much. But some nearby stars give a clue: measurements show that they are slowly changing their position with respect to the star patterns. All the stars in our galaxy are shooting through space at speeds of many miles per second, and the closer they are, the more noticeable this motion becomes.

THE CLOSEST STARS

star		constellation	magnitude app.	abs.	type	distance (l.y.)	proper motion ("/century)
Proxima		Centaurus	10·7	15·1	dwarf	4.3	387
Rigil	A	Centaurus	0·0	4·4	dwarf	4.3	367
Kent. (α)	B	Centaurus	1·4	5·8	dwarf	4.3	367
Barnard's star		Ophiuchus	9·5	13·2	dwarf	5.2	1,030
Wolf 359		Leo	13·5	16·7	dwarf	7.6	467
Lalande 21185		Ursa Major	7·5	10·5	dwarf	8.1	477
UV	A	Cetus	12·5	15·3	dwarf	8.4	336
	B	Cetus	13·0	15·8	dwarf	8.4	336
Sirius	A	Canis Major	-1·5	1·4	dwarf	8.7	307
(α)	B	Canis Major	8·5	11·4	white dwarf	8.7	307
Ross 154		Sagittarius	10·6	13·3	dwarf	9.5	74
Ross 248		Andromeda	12·2	14·7	dwarf	10.3	182
ϵ		Eridanus	3·7	6·1	dwarf	10.7	98
Ross 128		Virgo	11·1	13·5	dwarf	10.8	136
61	A	Cygnus	5·2	7·5	dwarf	11.1	520
	B	Cygnus	6·0	8·4	dwarf	11.1	520
L789-6		Aquarius	12·2	14·6	dwarf	11.2	327
ϵ		Indus	4·7	7·0	dwarf	11.2	469
BD+4344	A	Andromeda	8·1	10·4	dwarf	11.2	?
	B	Andromeda	11·1	13·4	dwarf	11.2	?
Procyon (α)	A	Canis Minor	0·3	2·6	subgiant	11.4	125
	B	Canis Minor	10·8	13·1	white dwarf	11.4	125

The letters "A" and "B" refer to the brighter and fainter members of a binary star system (see page 50).

▶ **Measuring a distance** by parallax. In the six months between Earth moving from its January to its July positions, stars A and B appear to shift against the distant background—the closer star B having shifted more. Knowing the distance from Earth to the Sun (the astronomical unit), each star's distance may be determined.

Earth-based parallaxes can be used for distances of up to 100 light-years or so, but the Hipparcos astrometry satellite (1989–1993) made accurate measurements for many more stars. Comparing a star's apparent and absolute magnitudes also gives a key to its distance.

star A
star B
Earth in July
Sun
Earth in January

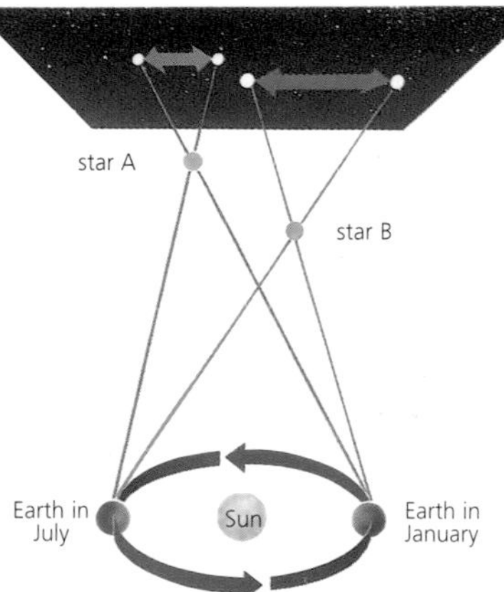

▼ **This diagram** shows the relative sizes of the Sun and its closest companion star, as well as three planets and the Moon. To represent the relative distances, however, they would have to be separated by the amounts shown, and the whole Earth could only accommodate a few of the Sun's neighbors.

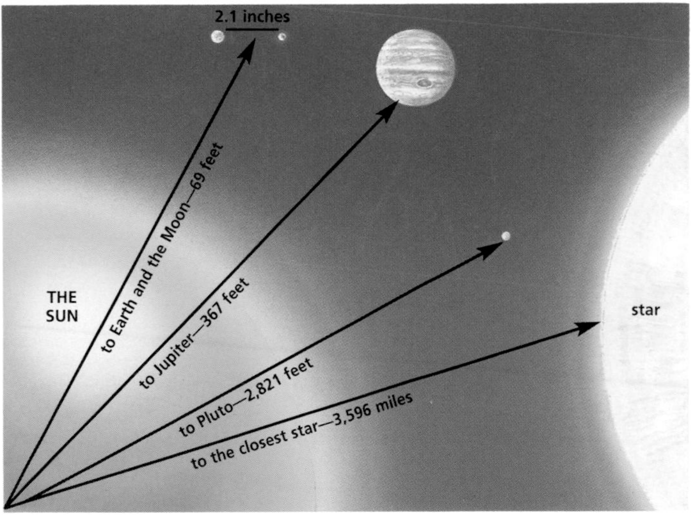

2.1 inches
to Earth and the Moon—69 feet
to Jupiter—367 feet
to Pluto—2,821 feet
to the closest star—3,596 miles
THE SUN
star

How the stars shine

Stars shine because of nuclear reactions deep inside their interiors. They are mostly made up of hydrogen gas. The tremendous pressure in their centers raises the temperature to millions of degrees, and in the heat the hydrogen atoms break down, recombining as helium. This releases enough energy to keep the process going as long as the hydrogen lasts.

But some stars are much hotter than others, and the color of a star depends on its temperature. White stars may have a surface temperature of 90,032°F; cool red stars may be below 5,432°F. The Sun, at 9,932°F, is yellowish.

A color-magnitude (or Hertzprung-Russell) diagram, shown on the opposite page, plots surface temperatures against absolute magnitudes, and star families emerge. The most important is the *main sequence*, where most stars are found; they are known as *dwarfs*, to distinguish them from the inflated *giants* and *supergiants*. The *white dwarfs*, on the other hand, are small and dense and are so dim that very few have been discovered, although they almost certainly outnumber the giants.

The color-magnitude diagram is like a photograph of a crowd of people—it shows the differences between individuals. It took astronomers a long time to realize how these various types of stars are related. At first they thought that stars traveled along the main sequence as they developed. The current belief is that stars like the Sun originate to the right of the main sequence, spend most of their life at one point on it, inflate into the red giant domain, and then quickly cross it on their way to the white dwarf state at the bottom left.

▶ **HERTZSPRUNG-RUSSELL DIAGRAM**
Bright stars are often given a special name of their own such as Sirius. Others are known by a Greek letter or a number, followed by the Latin genitive form of a constellation name. In the diagram on the right, for example, we find ε Eridani (star ε in the constellation Eridanus) and 61 Cygni (star 61 in the constellation Cygnus). The Greek alphabet is given on page 50. A few unusual stars are named after the astronomer who examined them such as Barnard's star.

THE STELLAR SPECTRUM

If starlight is passed through a spectroscope —a device used to broaden it into a colored band—several dark lines are usually seen. The colored band is produced by the star's shining surface, while the dark lines indicate narrow strips of color that have been absorbed by elements in its thin surrounding atmosphere.

By matching their lines with those obtained in a laboratory, astronomers can discover what elements are present in the star's atmosphere. However, the element helium was detected in the Sun before it was discovered on Earth.

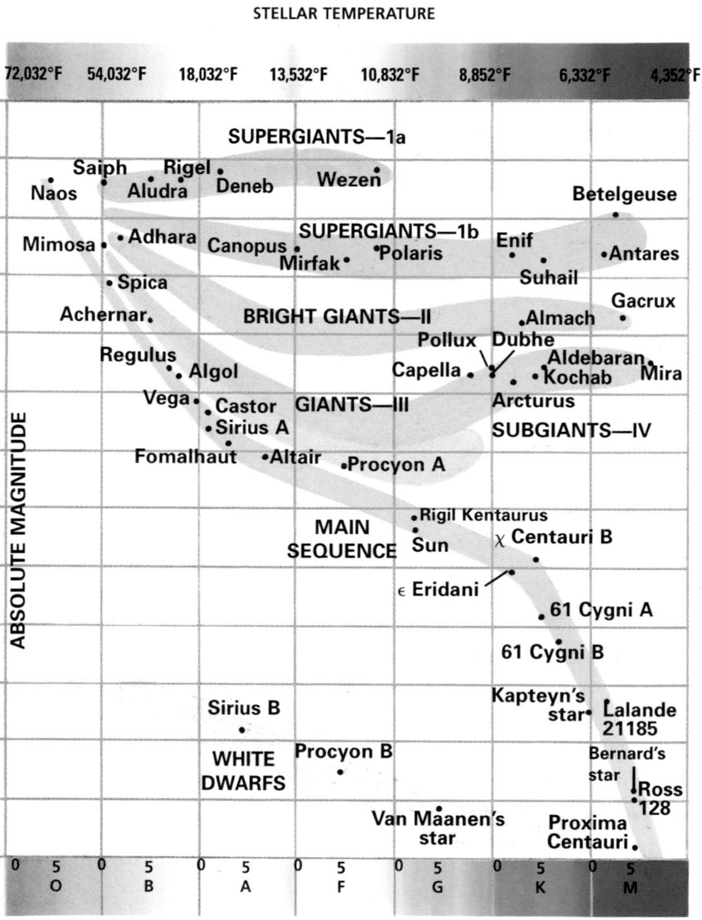

STELLAR TEMPERATURE

72,032°F 54,032°F 18,032°F 13,532°F 10,832°F 8,852°F 6,332°F 4,352°F

ABSOLUTE MAGNITUDE

SUPERGIANTS—1a

Saiph Rigel Naos Aludra Deneb Wezen Betelgeuse

SUPERGIANTS—1b

Mimosa Adhara Canopus Mirfak Polaris Enif Suhail Antares

Spica

Achernar BRIGHT GIANTS—II Almach Gacrux

Pollux Dubhe

Regulus Algol Capella Aldebaran Kochab Mira

Vega Castor GIANTS—III Arcturus

Sirius A SUBGIANTS—IV

Fomalhaut Altair Procyon A

Rigil Kentaurus

MAIN SEQUENCE Sun χ Centauri B

ϵ Eridani

61 Cygni A

61 Cygni B

Kapteyn's star Lalande 21185

Sirius B

WHITE DWARFS Procyon B Bernard's star Ross 128

Van Maanen's star Proxima Centauri

0 5 O 0 5 B 0 5 A 0 5 F 0 5 G 0 5 K 0 5 M

The life and death of a star

Stars form from clouds of dust and gas, called nebulae, that make up a high proportion of the material that is found in normal galaxies. When it becomes dense enough, the nebula goes "critical" and starts to condense into numerous clouds that are dark to begin with but heat up and begin to shine as stars. The temperature and brightness of the star depends on the mass of the cloud.

Most stars, like the Sun, start the main part of their life as main-sequence stars. But as they burn their hydrogen, their cores become hotter, and they emit shells of relatively cool gas: they have evolved into red giants, like Aldebaran. Eventually the shell disappears, and only the intensely hot white core remains: the star is now a white dwarf, like Sirius B. A bright star, like Deneb, evolves in a few million years, whereas the much dimmer Sun will remain on the main sequence for billions of years.

► **A normal star** condenses from a dark cloud. It shines steadily for a long time, then expands into a red giant, and dies away as a tiny white dwarf. A massive star may end its life in a supernova explosion.

▼ **The Sun** is an ordinary main-sequence star. Hydrogen atoms are turned into helium atoms in its searing core, releasing enormous amounts of energy.

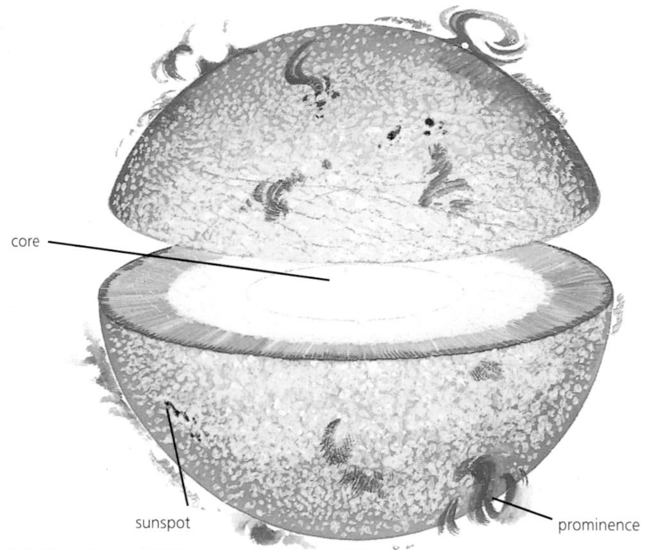

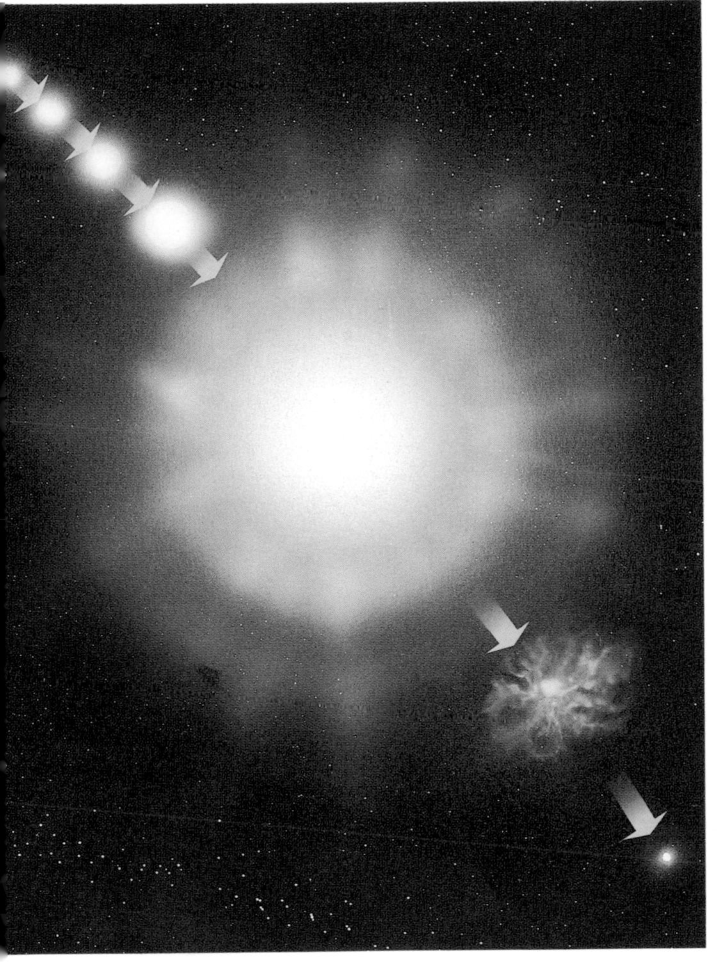

The stars

If you look at star Zeta (ζ) in the constellation Ursa Major (star map 1, pages 66 to 67), you will notice a fainter star, Alcor, close to it. This is a naked-eye double star. Turn a small astronomical telescope onto it, and Zeta itself (usually known as Mizar) is seen to be a close double.

The Mizar-Alcor pair is known as an *optical* double; the stars are far apart, and they just happen to be in almost the same direction. But Mizar is a true *binary*, and the stars are revolving around each other, although they may take around 14,000 years to achieve a revolution. The brighter star in a binary is known as the *primary*; the fainter as the *secondary*.

WELL-KNOWN DOUBLE STARS

constellation	name	magnitudes		separation (" arc)
Andromeda	Gamma γ	2·3	5·1	9.8
Boötes	Epsilon ε	2·5	4·9	2.8
Cancer	Zeta ζ	5·1	6·2	6.0
Cassiopeia	Iota ι	4·6	6·9	2.5
Centaurus	Alpha α	0·0	1·3	14.1
Centaurus	Gamma γ	2·9	2·9	1.0
Crux	Alpha α	1·3	1·7	4.4
Cygnus	Beta β	3·1	5·1	34.4
Hercules	Zeta ζ	2·9	5·5	0.8
Leo	Gamma γ	2·2	3·5	4.4
Monoceros	Epsilon ε	4·5	6·5	13.4
Orion	Iota ι	1·9	4·0	2.3
Scorpius	Beta β	2·6	4·9	13.6
Ursa Major	Zeta γ	2·3	4·0	14.4
Ursa Minor	Alpha α	2·0	9·0	18.4
Vela	Gamma γ	1·9	4·2	41.2
Virgo	Gamma γ	3·5	3·5	1.8

If the two stars are of different brightnesses, one eclipse is much deeper than the other (right). If they are similar, the eclipses resemble each other more closely (below right).

The distance between components of a double star is measured in seconds of arc ("). There are 60" in one minute of arc ('), and 60' equals one degree. An ordinary human hair, viewed from 40 feet (12m), is around one inch thick. Good binoculars can separate normal double stars whose components are only 30" apart. The well-known double Beta Cygni (page 81) is an excellent test object for northern observers. If one star is much brighter than the other, its companion will be difficult to see because it may be hidden by the glare.

The table above lists examples of double stars, ranging from easy binocular objects to much closer pairs that will require a good telescope and high magnification in order to be seen.

LETTERING THE STARS

The brighter stars in each constellation are given a Greek letter in approximate order of brightness, beginning with α. Since a number of these bright stars are important doubles, the Greek alphabet is given here.

α alpha	η eta	ν nu	τ tau
β beta	θ theta	ξ xi	υ upsilon
γ gamma	ι iota	ο omicron	φ phi
δ delta	κ kappa	π pi	χ chi
ε epsilon	λ lambda	ρ rho	ψ psi
ζ zeta	μ mu	σ sigma	ω omega

Eclipsing binaries

In some binary systems the two stars are so close that no telescope can separate them. They can only be detected by double lines in the spectrum, or by one star eclipsing the other. The eclipse effect will only be noticed if the orbit appears almost edge-on, as seen from Earth.

Beta Persei (Algol) is an example of an *eclipsing binary*, consisting of a bright star and a dim star. In the diagram on the right light from both stars reaches Earth (1). After around 18 hours (2) the dim star partly blocks off the bright star, and the total magnitude drops. At (3), one and a half days later, there is a slight brightness drop as the dim star is obstructed.

Another naked-eye eclipsing binary, Beta Lyrae, consists of two equal stars almost touching. The diagram below shows that its light change is continuous. These two binary systems represent the *dark-eclipsing* and *bright-eclipsing* families of variable stars, and hundreds of members are known.

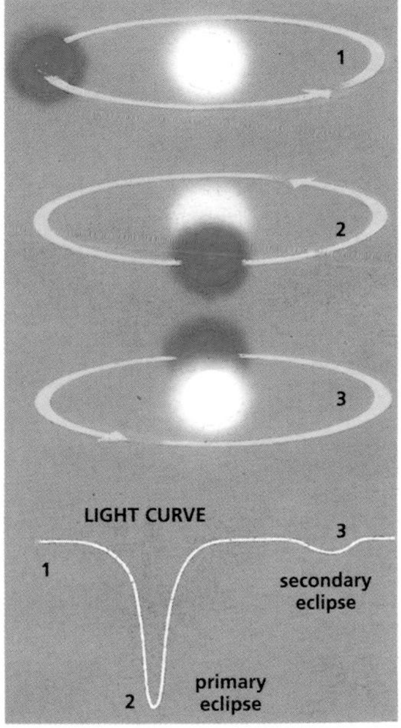

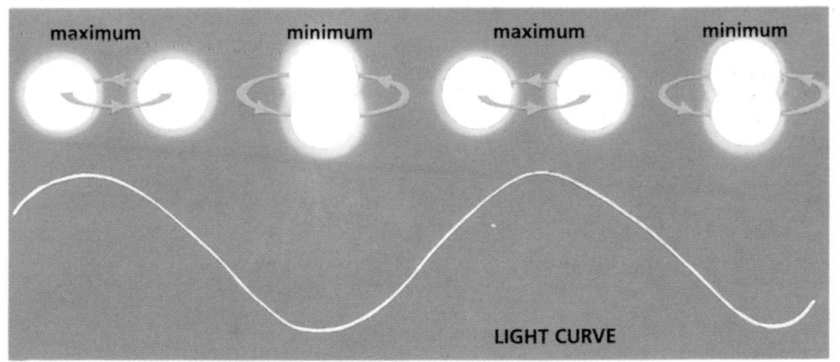

Variable stars

Eclipsing binaries are known as *extrinsic variables*, since the stars themselves do not change in brightness. *Intrinsic variables* actually change in luminosity, usually due to huge pulsations.

One well-known group is the *Cepheid* family, so-named because the first one was discovered in the constellation Cepheus. These are yellow supergiant stars that brighten and fade by up to two magnitudes in a regular pattern. Cepheids are important, since their mean absolute magnitude is related to their period. By timing a Cepheid, its absolute magnitude can be determined. By comparing its absolute magnitude with its apparent magnitude, its distance can then be found.

Long-period variables (LPVs) form a very large group. They are red giant stars with much longer periods than Cepheids.

These range from around 200 to 500 days and vary by up to ten magnitudes in brightness. They do not repeat themselves exactly from cycle to cycle. A famous long-period variable, Mira in Cetus, shows dramatic changes in its brightness; it has appeared almost as bright as the North Star, while at its minimum it is barely visible with ordinary binoculars. Stars of this type are known as Mira stars.

▼ **Cepheid variables** repeat their brightness variations exactly from cycle to cycle, although some vary in brightness more than others. More luminous stars have longer periods.

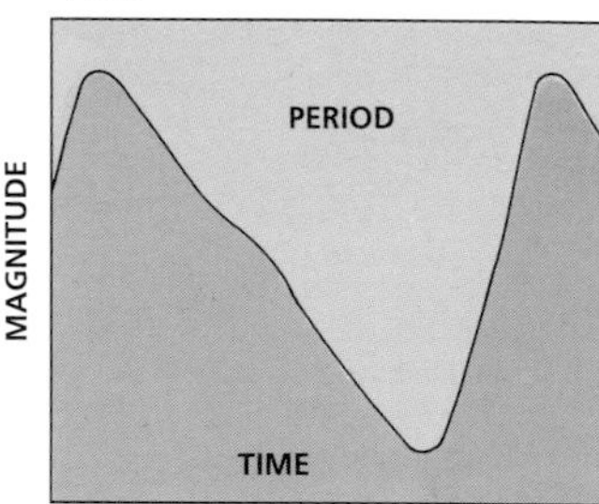

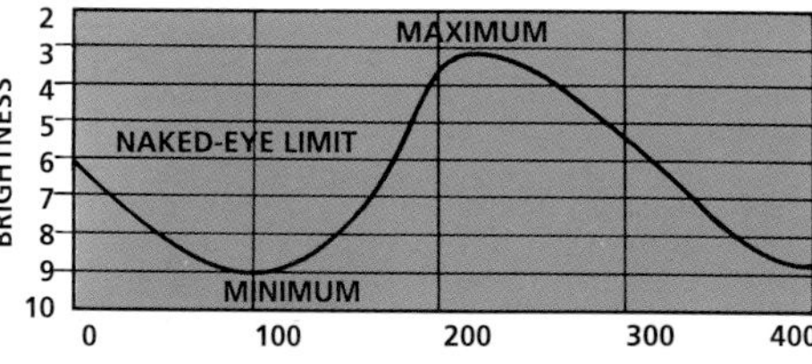

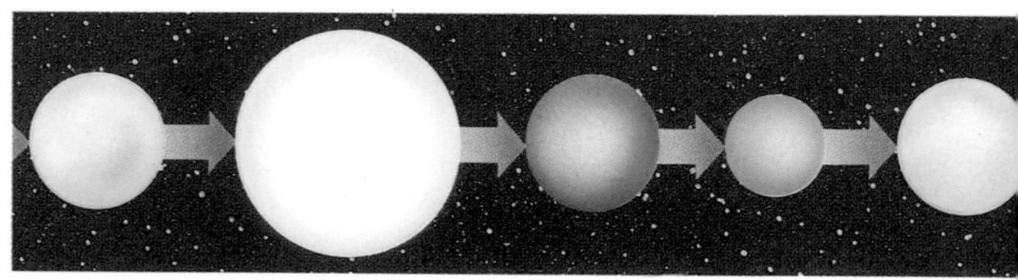

Observing variable stars

Variable star observation is very popular with amateur astronomers. It consists of estimating the star's magnitude by comparing it with nearby *comparison stars*, whose magnitudes are known. There are several ways of making an estimate.

One way is to locate two comparison stars—one brighter than the variable, and the other fainter—and to decide how the variable "fits" between them. It may be exactly midway in brightness or closer to one or the other. With skill and experience, estimates can be accurate to 0·2 magnitude or even less. This is called the *fractional* method.

You can also try the *step* method, learning to recognize steps of 0·1 magnitude and estimating by how many steps the variable differs from a comparison star.

Some advanced amateurs are now using electronic equipment to measure the brightness of variable stars. Accuracy of 0·01 magnitude is possible, but for many stars this precision level is not necessary. For example, a family of stars known as dwarf novas spend most of their time at minimum brightness, but will suddenly rise by several tenths of a magnitude overnight. Other stars spend most of their time at their maximum and then plunge by several magnitudes in a few weeks.

This work is important, since professional astronomers cannot observe all the variable stars, and amateur-professional links are now well established. Variable star methods can also be used to estimate the brightness of small solar system objects such as comets and minor planets.

◀ **This light curve** of a long-period variable star (*o* Ceti, or Mira), shows how it rose and fell in brightness.

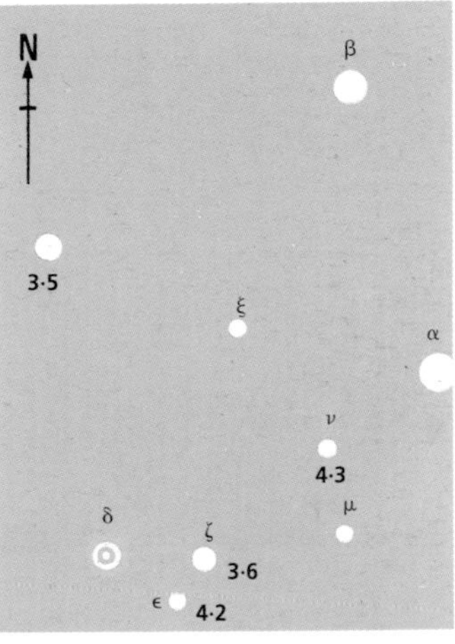

▲ **This chart** shows the brighter stars in Cepheus (page 79), with comparison stars for the famous variable δ (Delta).

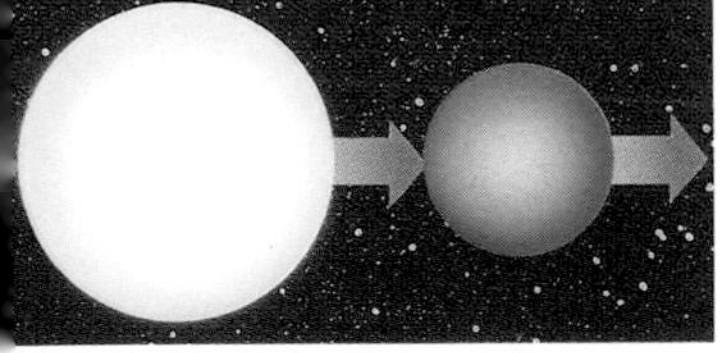

◀ **Mira stars** are a family of adolescent red giants, caught in a brief expanding and contracting phase as the star "evolves" off the main sequence to become a red giant. Eventually the Sun may become a Mira star.

Novas and supernovas

Some variable stars are unpredictable and violent. Every few years a new naked-eye star suddenly shines out, literally overnight. This is a *nova*—a member of a close binary system that blasts off a huge shell of material. A nova can rise in brightness by more than 10,000 times in a couple of days.

Some amateurs hunt for novas, scanning the Milky Way with binoculars. The most successful of this group, G. E. D. Alcock of Peterborough, England, found five novas between 1967 and 1991. To discover a nova, you must know the sky really well, so that a single extra star is quickly noticed.

Supernovas are even rarer. This is the complete self-destruction of a massive star, and it rivals an entire galaxy in its brightness. In 1987 a supernova in the Large Magellanic Cloud—a companion galaxy to our own Milky Way—could be seen with the naked eye. The previous nearby supernova occurred in 1604! All but the core of the star is blasted into space when the supernova explodes. This forms a neutron star, or a black hole (see page 154).

VARIABLE STAR TYPES

star	magnitude range	period	map no.
eclipsing binaries			
ϵ Aurigae	3·0–4·0	27.1 years	3
ζ Aurigae	3·8–4·3	972 days	3
β Lyrae	3·3–4·2	12.9 days	7
β Persei (Algol)	2·2–3·2	69 hours	3
Cepheid variables			
η Aquilae	4·1–5·4	7.2 days	7
δ Cephei	3·5–4·3	5.4 days	1
β Doradus	3·8–4·8	9.8 days	8
long-period variables			
o Ceti (Mira)	3–10	330 days	2
χ Cygni	4–14	406 days	7
irregular variables			
ρ Cassiopeiae	4–6		1
μ Cephei	4–5		1
ϵ Herculls (Rasalgethi)	3–4		6
α Orionis (Betelgeuse)	0·4–1·3	5 years?	3
α Scorpii (Antares)	0·9–1·8	5 years?	6
other variables			
γ Cassiopeiae	1·7–2·4	(usually faint)	1
T Coronae Borealis	2–10	(usually faint)	6
R Coronae Borealis	6–14	(usually bright)	6

▲ **The Crab Nebula** is the remains of a supernova that was seen in 1054, equivalent in violence to one million million million million hydrogen bombs.

▼ **The remnant of a supernova** that was thought to have occurred in 1657. This explosion involved a massive star that weighed almost 100 times more than the Sun.

Nebulae and star clusters

The word *nebula* means cloud, and there are many cloudy-looking objects in the sky. But any comparison with terrestrial clouds is misleading. 35 cubic feet ($1m^3$) of rain cloud weighs around four ounces (100g), but a volume of nebula the size of Earth would weigh less than ten pounds! Nebulae are only noticeable because they are so huge.

A nebula, like almost everything in the universe, mostly consists of hydrogen, although compounds of hydrogen with nitrogen, carbon, oxygen, and other elements may be found. There are four main types of nebulae:

Planetary nebulae are shells of gas that are expelled from very hot stars. They are called planetary nebulae

The Ring Nebula (below) was expelled from a star. The Horsehead (above) and Orion Nebula (left) indicate where young stars are forming.

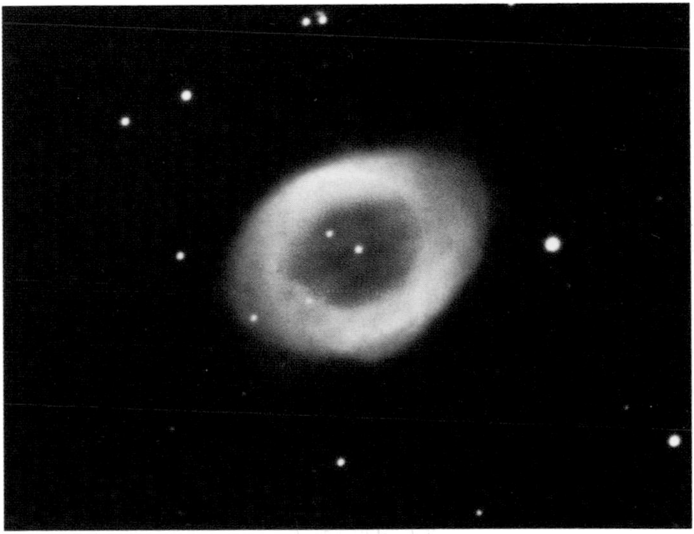

because some of them appear disklike in small telescopes. They are usually relatively small—less than one light-year across. Most of them are very faint. An example is M57 in Lyra (star map 7).

Reflection nebulae shine by reflected starlight, and they are usually faint. An example is the Pleiades in Taurus (star map 3).

Emission nebulae are huge, irregular clouds that are tens of light-years across, and stars form within them. They shine because their atoms react with radiation from nearby hot stars. An example is M8 in Sagittarius (star map 7).

Dark nebulae can only be detected by what they obscure. The Milky Way outline is irregular because of dark nebulae in front of the stars. An example is M42 in Orion (star map 3).

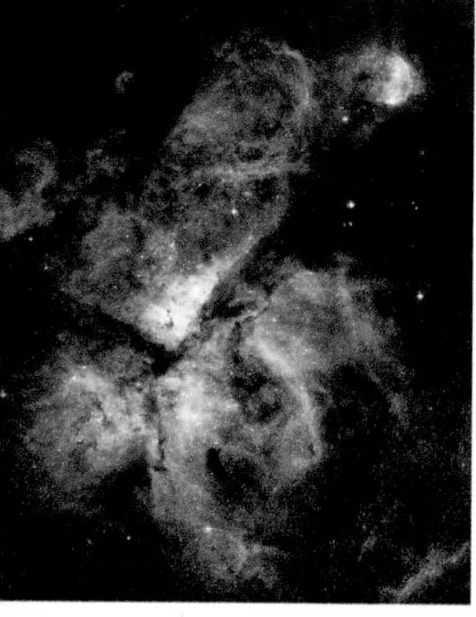

Star clusters

Stars form in clusters rather than as individuals, condensing out of separate clouds within a nebula that is many light-years across. Presumably the Sun was once a cluster member. But every star has a separate motion of its own, and unless the cluster is very compact so that the gravitational pull of its members holds the group together, the stars drift apart over many millions of years.

These *open* clusters are being born all the time. For example, young stars are being formed in the Orion Nebula, M42. Clusters are very interesting to astronomers, since the stars in them form a mixed group of types, all of them the same age. Around 300 open clusters have been discovered in our galaxy.

A cluster's probable age can be determined by examining its population. If it contains many very hot stars, it must be young—since such stars burn out quickly or evolve into red giants. If it contains red giants and white dwarfs, it must be old.

Open clusters occur throughout the arms of our galaxy, but *globular* clusters are completely different. They are about as old as our galaxy itself and contain red giant stars. They measure up to 100 light-years across, and their population

◀ **The Keyhole Nebula** is currently giving birth to a cluster of stars.

▶ **The Pleiades** are a young cluster—probably less than 100 million years old. The six or seven brightest stars are detectable with the naked eye: they are white giant stars that are thousands of times as luminous as the Sun. They have not had time to evolve; so far there are neither red giants nor white dwarfs.

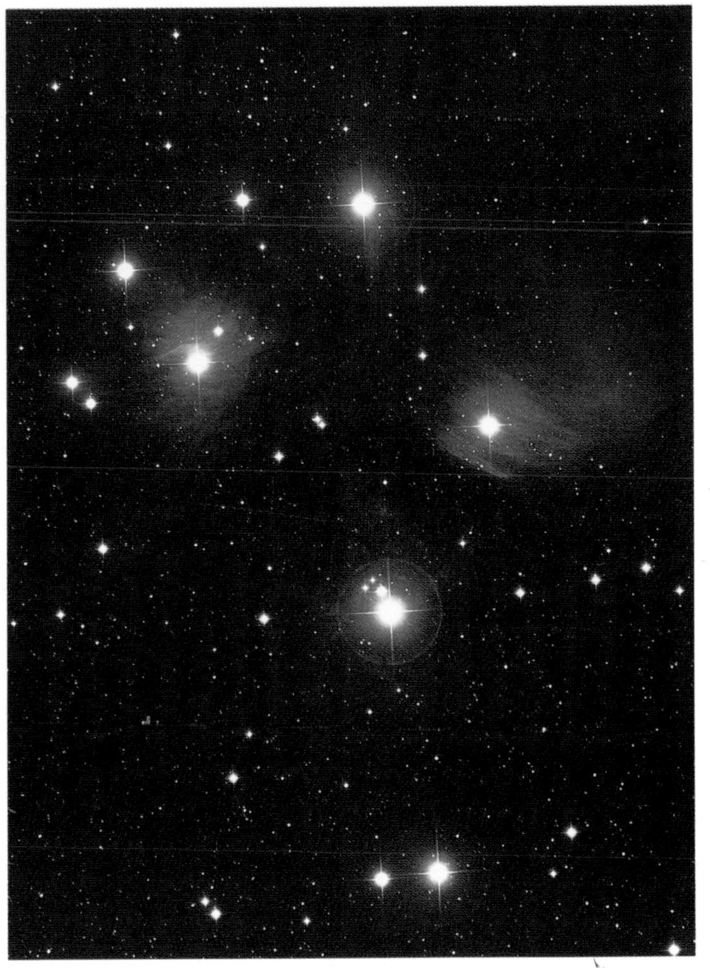

is determined in hundreds of thousands of stars. There are around 150 globular clusters in our galaxy and many more in some other galaxies. They form a "halo" around our star system.

Observing star clusters

The brightest open and globular clusters can be seen with the naked eye, as long as the sky is very dark. Binoculars will give a good view of some of the larger open clusters. With apertures from 60 to 150 millimeters, many are excellent. Even experienced amateurs never get tired of these objects.

You should remember that photographs that are taken with large telescopes show much more detail in clusters and nebulae than may be visible to the naked eye, even when you are using a large instrument. On the other hand, no photograph can capture the telescopic brilliance of stars sparkling in the eyepiece.

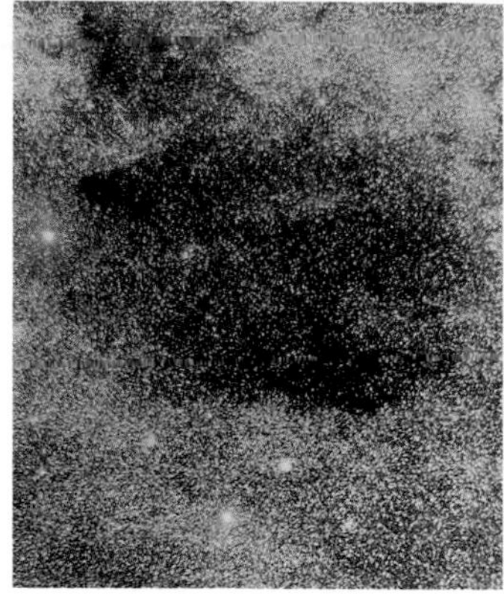

▲ **The Coal Sack Nebula** obscures stars in the Milky Way.

▼ **Omega Centauri**, the finest globular cluster in the sky, lies far south of the celestial equator. It is easily visible with the naked eye.

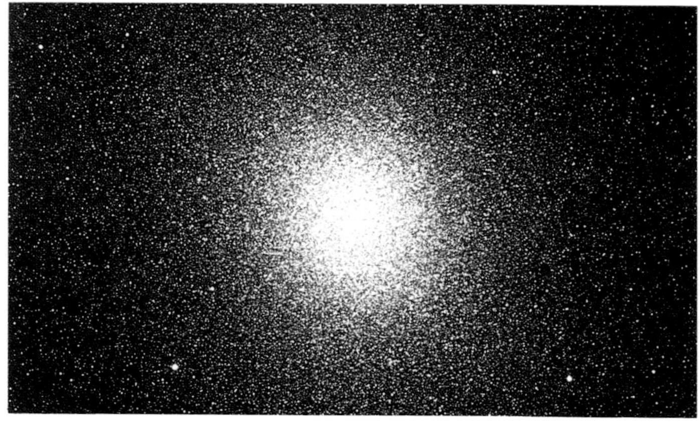

The constellations

The constellations are imaginary groupings of the stars. Invented many years ago by people to help map out the sky, they are still the easiest way to learn the stars. This chapter describes the most interesting of the 88 constellations, all of which are shown on the maps. The brighter or more important stars are identified by name or by letter. The standard three-letter abbreviation of each constellation is also given with each entry.

The stars are roughly grouped together according to brightness—the largest circles representing the brightest stars. Being careful to stay out of all direct light, the faintest stars shown here should be visible with the naked eye from suburban sites.

Nebulae and star clusters, as well as galaxies, are given an "M" number from Messier's 1781 catalog (for example, the Orion Nebula, M42), or a number only from the New General Catalog (NGC) of 1888 (for example, the Double Cluster in Perseus, 869 and 884).

USING THE STAR MAPS

The maps on pages 66–75 represent the entire celestial sphere divided into six segments, plus the northern and southern circumpolar regions, as shown below. The areas that are covered by each map, allowing for some overlap in RA, are as follows:

1 dec +50° to N. Pole
2 RA 22 hrs.–2 hrs.
3 RA 2 hrs.–6 hrs.
4 RA 6 hrs.–10 hrs.
5 RA 10 hrs.–14 hrs.
6 RA 14 hrs.–18 hrs.
7 RA 18 hrs.–22 hrs.
8 dec -50° to S. Pole

(2–7: dec +50° to -50°)

The maps show all the stars in the sky, down to around magnitude 4·5, as well as the positions of clusters, nebulae, etc., usually known as "deep-sky objects."

These deep-sky objects are usually much fainter than the stars shown on the maps. Some special charts, to help locate the more difficult objects, have been added to the constellation notes.

There are also special charts for variable stars, which give the magnitudes of suitable comparison stars.

The light blue strip shows the path of the Milky Way and some of the more obvious irregularities in its course.

"h" represents "hours"

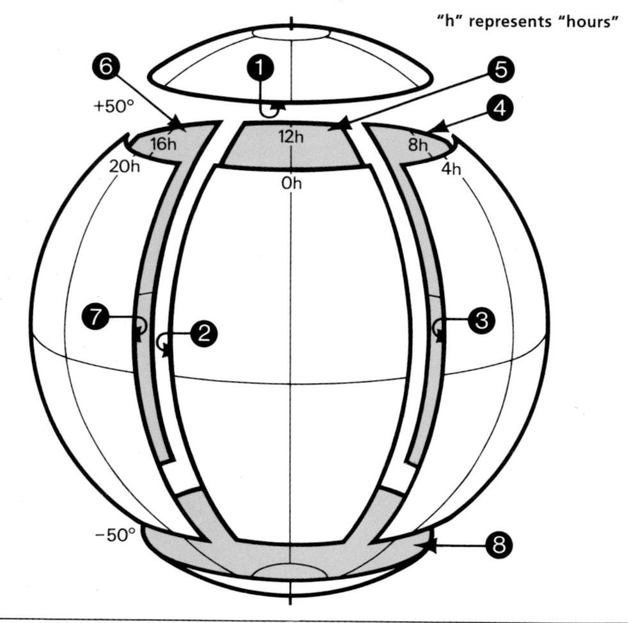

Finding a star

Star maps can be very confusing at first. It is difficult to compare the stars shown flat on paper to the arc of stars in the sky above. A good way to avoid disappointment is to learn to look for some of the brighter stars. Once you are familiar with these, the other patterns will be easier to find.

The constellations of Ursa Major and Orion are so well known that they can be used to identify other stars and groups. Ursa Major is always in the northern part of the sky, and it is circumpolar for much of Europe and the U.S. Orion lies on the celestial equator and is visible everywhere in the world between September and April. The region of Ursa Major is shown on star maps 1 (pages 66–67) and 5 (page 71), while Orion appears on star map 3 (page 69).

The diagrams on this page show how to use different star alignments in these two constellations. A more systematic method is described below.

ORION

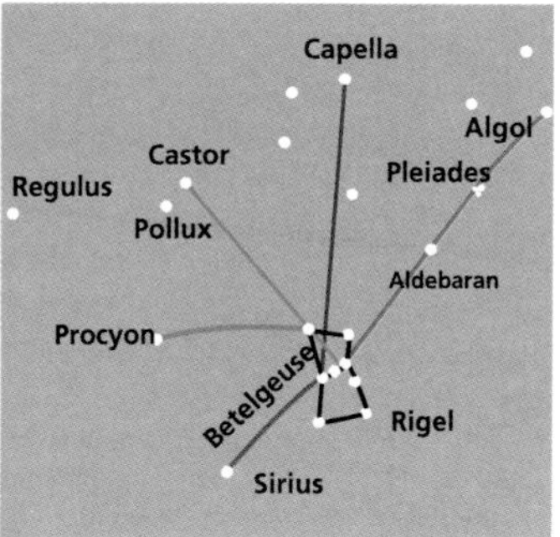

URSA MAJOR

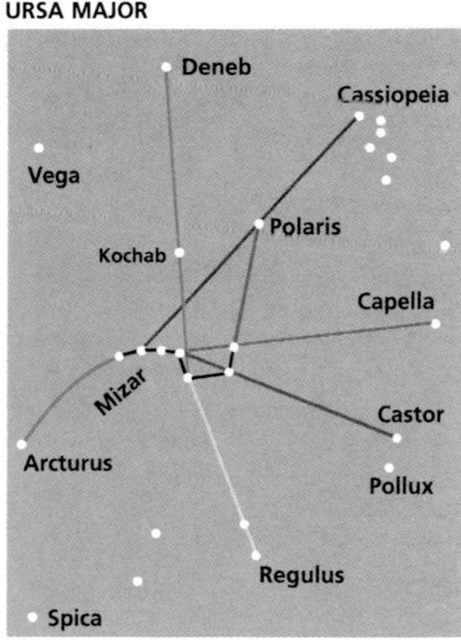

Where to look

All celestial objects are at their highest when they are crossing the *meridian* (the north-south line that passes overhead). Unless the object is close to the celestial pole, it will be due south to a northern observer, and due north to a southern one.

Take the dec of the brightest star in the constellation from the notes that follow the star maps. Also, find out the colatitude of your site (the colatitude is equal to 90° minus your latitude).

Add the star's dec to this amount, and the result is the star's altitude above the horizon as it crosses the meridian. This is the angle to which you must set your alidade.

Don't forget that if the star has a

ST is about

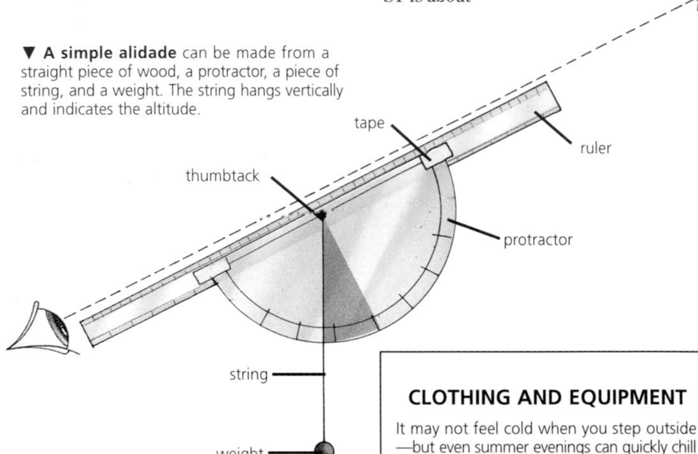

▼ **A simple alidade** can be made from a straight piece of wood, a protractor, a piece of string, and a weight. The string hangs vertically and indicates the altitude.

> **CLOTHING AND EQUIPMENT**
>
> It may not feel cold when you step outside —but even summer evenings can quickly chill enthusiasm if you are not adequately dressed.
>
> Good dark-adaptation is also essential. The eyes take at least ten minutes to acclimatize, so make sure that you have not left anything vital in a brightly-lit room.
>
> Work with a dim red light. A bicycle rear light may be too bright. Try painting most of an ordinary flashlight with red poster paint.

southern dec, you subtract the number from the complement. If you live south of the equator, call south dec positive and north dec negative and add and subtract accordingly.

Timing observations

As well as knowing *where* to look, you must know *when* to look. As Earth turns, objects are carried past the meridian. The sidereal time (ST) gives the RA that is on the meridian at any moment.

For example, Regulus (Alpha Leonis) is at RA 10 hrs. 6 mins., so it is on the meridian just after 10 hrs. ST. To convert ST to GMT, for an observer standing on the Greenwich meridian, use the converter on page 65. For example, if you are observing on January 31, 10 hrs. 6 mins., ST is about the same as 1 hr. 30 mins. GMT, or 1:30 A.M., so Regulus is on the meridian at this time. (Note that GMT is used in the U.K., but observers in other parts of the world use their own local time system.) A better time to observe Leo would be in March; March 31, for example, Regulus will be on the meridian at 21:30 GMT (9:30 P.M.).

Once you have identified a few of the brighter groups, the fainter constellations can be fit into the gaps easily, using the such as *Norton's Star Atlas* (see page 172), until you know the letters of all the naked-eye stars. If it is a Milky Way constellation, keep an eye out for a nova.

Very few amateurs have ever bothered to learn more than around 20 bright "signpost" stars. But if you make an effort and observe systematically, you can memorize hundreds of stars.

Finally, buy a notebook and record all you learn and see (or fail to see!). You will treasure it later, and some of the information may be valuable in years to come. Include the date and time with all your observations.

▼ **Use this diagram** to determine when a star of known RA will be on the meridian (GMT).

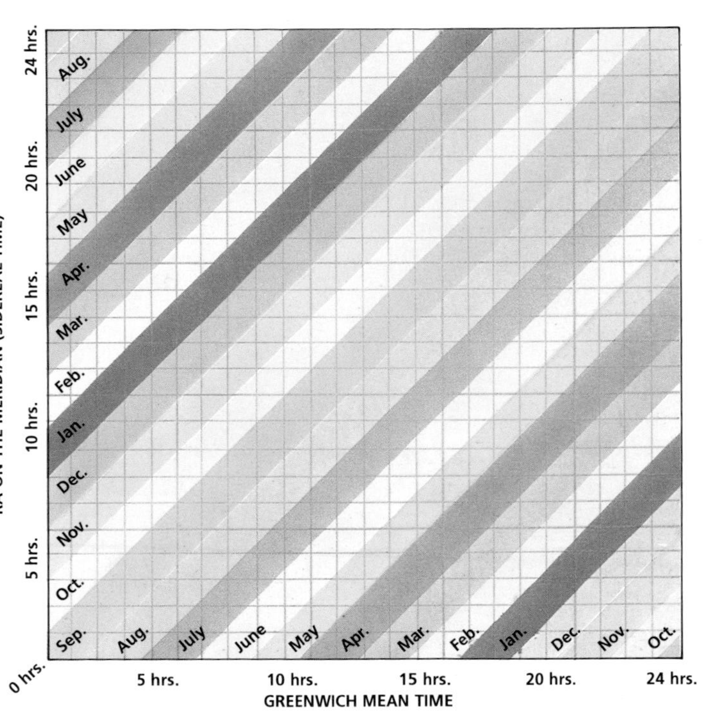

STAR MAP 1: Northern circumpolar stars

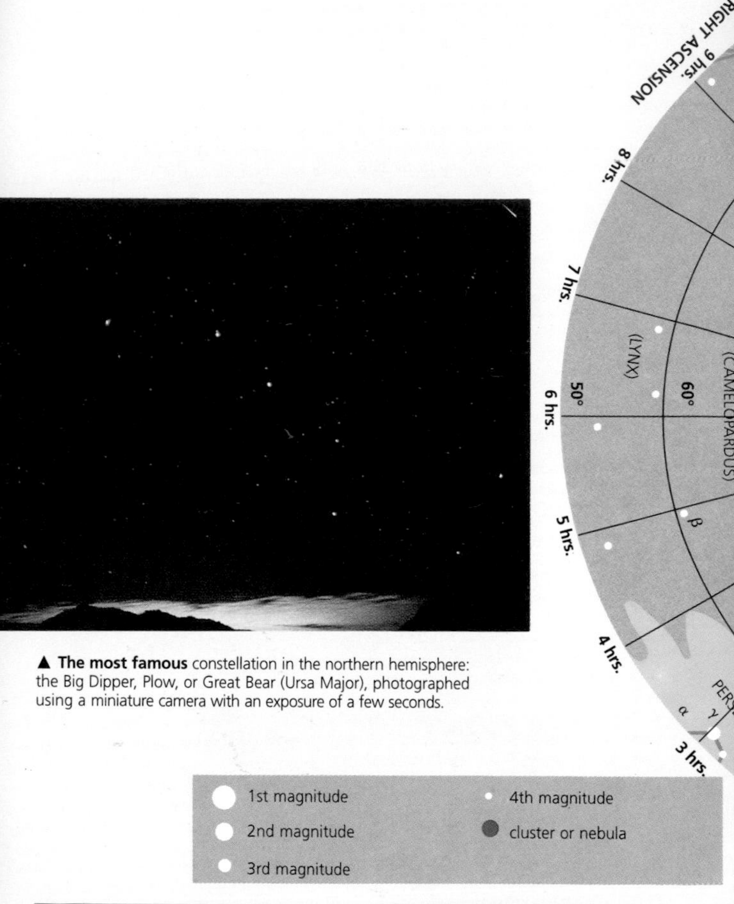

▲ **The most famous** constellation in the northern hemisphere: the Big Dipper, Plow, or Great Bear (Ursa Major), photographed using a miniature camera with an exposure of a few seconds.

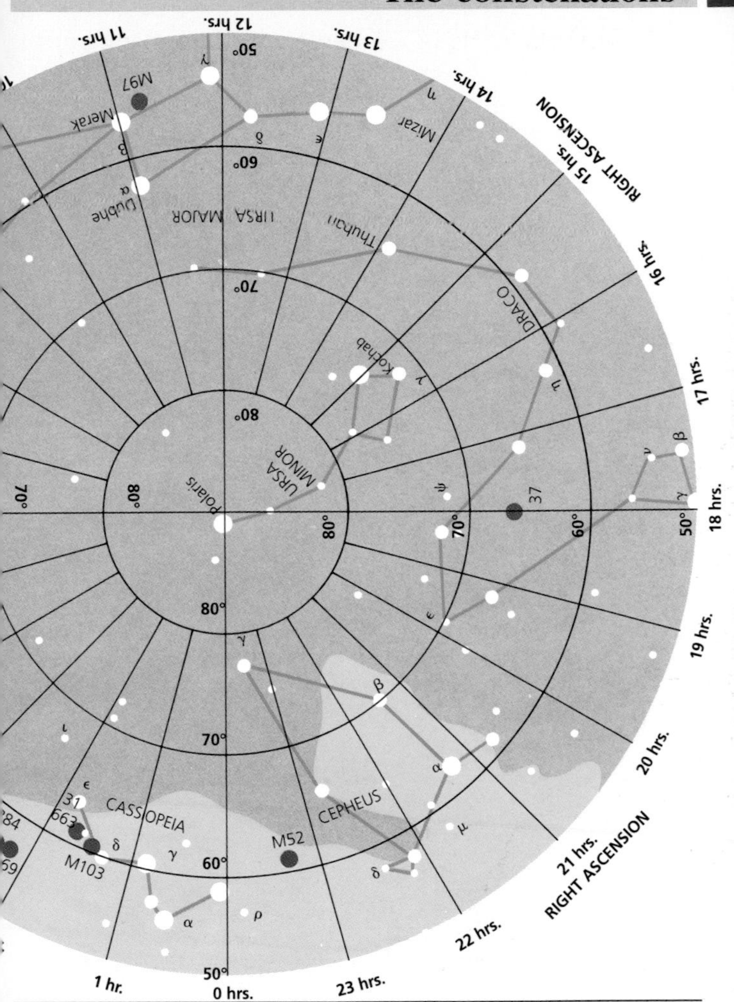

12 hrs.
11 hrs.
13 hrs.
14 hrs.
15 hrs.
16 hrs.
17 hrs.
18 hrs.
19 hrs.
20 hrs.
21 hrs.
22 hrs.
23 hrs.
0 hrs.
1 hr.
RIGHT ASCENSION
RIGHT ASCENSION
50°
60°
70°
80°
M97
Merak
Dubhe
Mizar
URSA MAJOR
Thuban
DRACO
Kochab
URSA MINOR
Polaris
37
CEPHEUS
CASSIOPEIA
M52
M103
663
31

STAR MAP 2: Right ascension 22 hours–2 hours

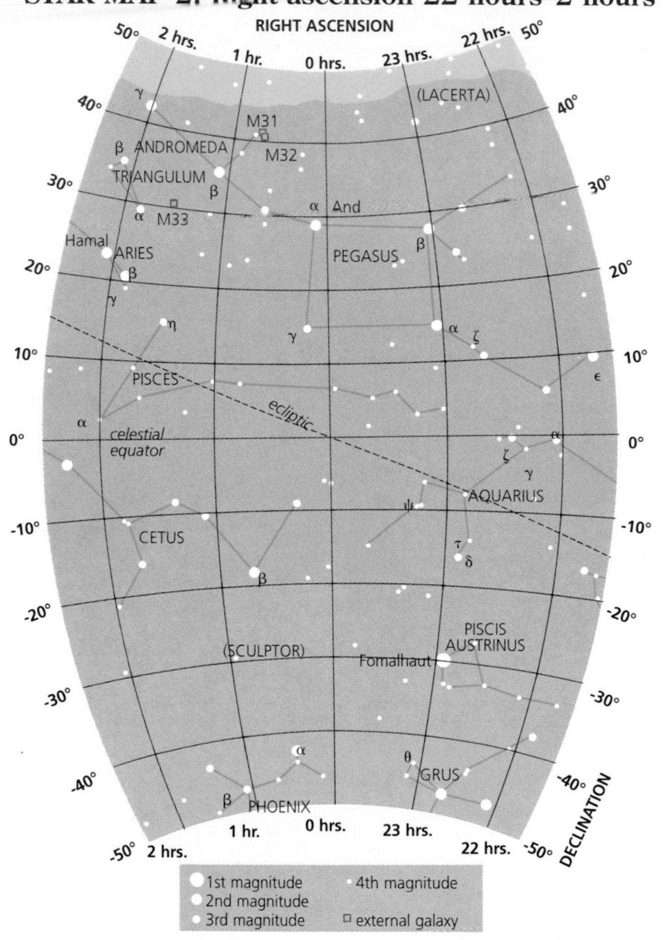

STAR MAP 3: Right ascension 2 hours–6 hours

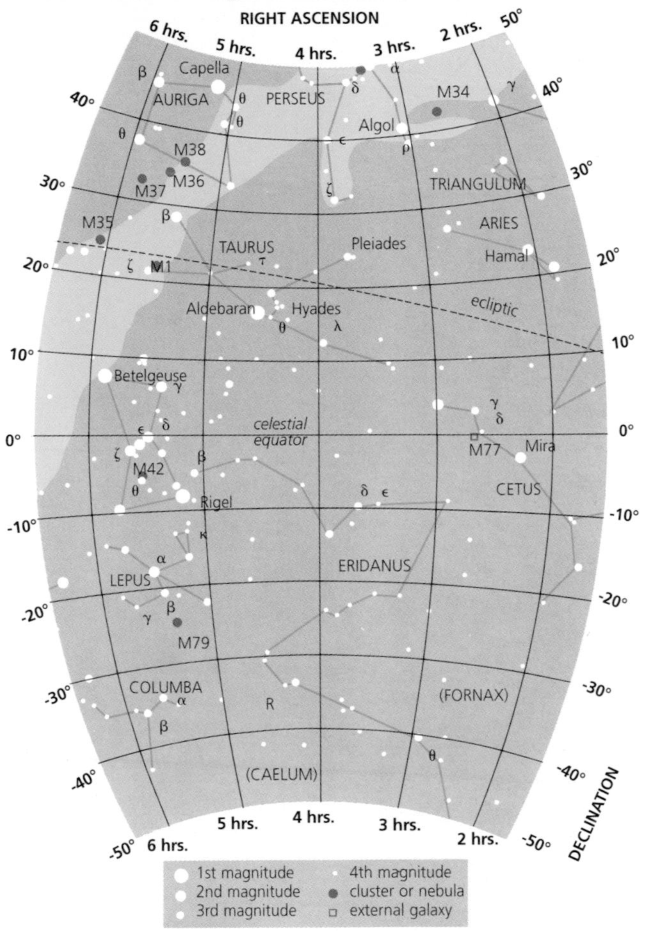

STAR MAP 4: Right ascension 6 hours–10 hours

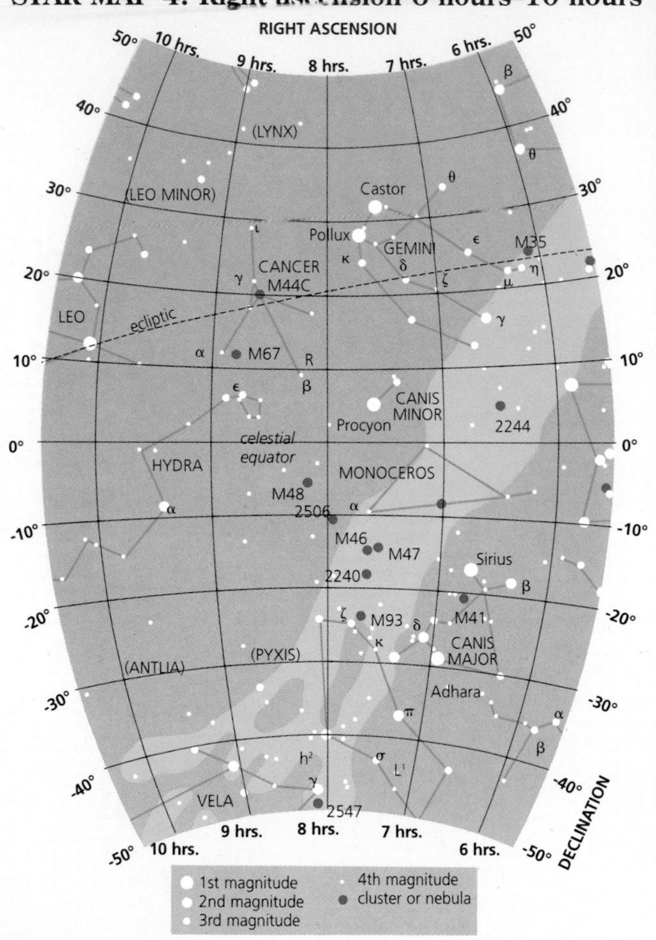

STAR MAP 5: Right ascension 10 hours–14 hours

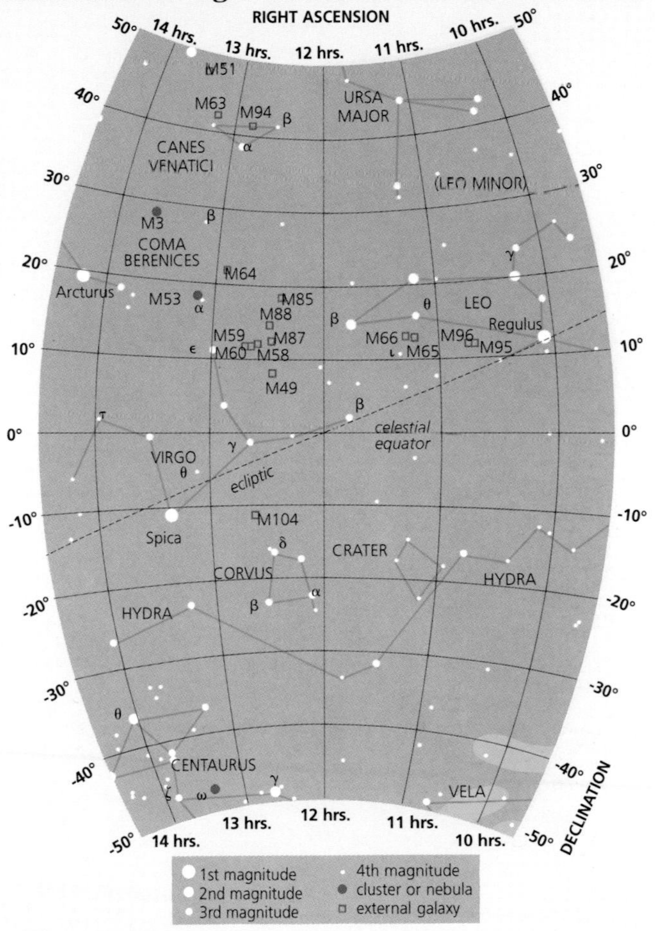

STAR MAP 6: Right ascension 14 hours–18 hours

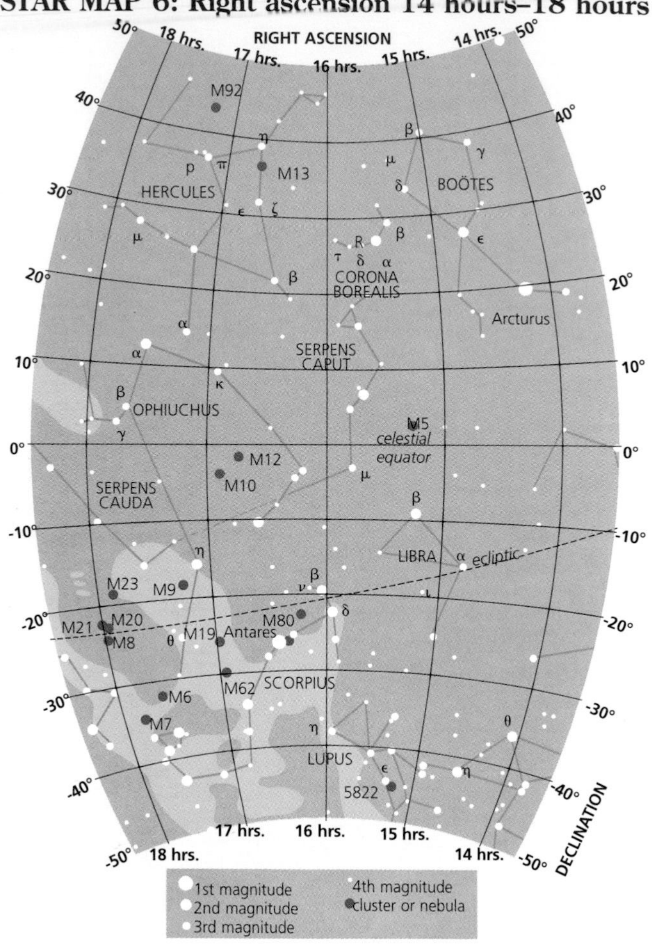

STAR MAP 7: Right ascension 18 hours–22 hours

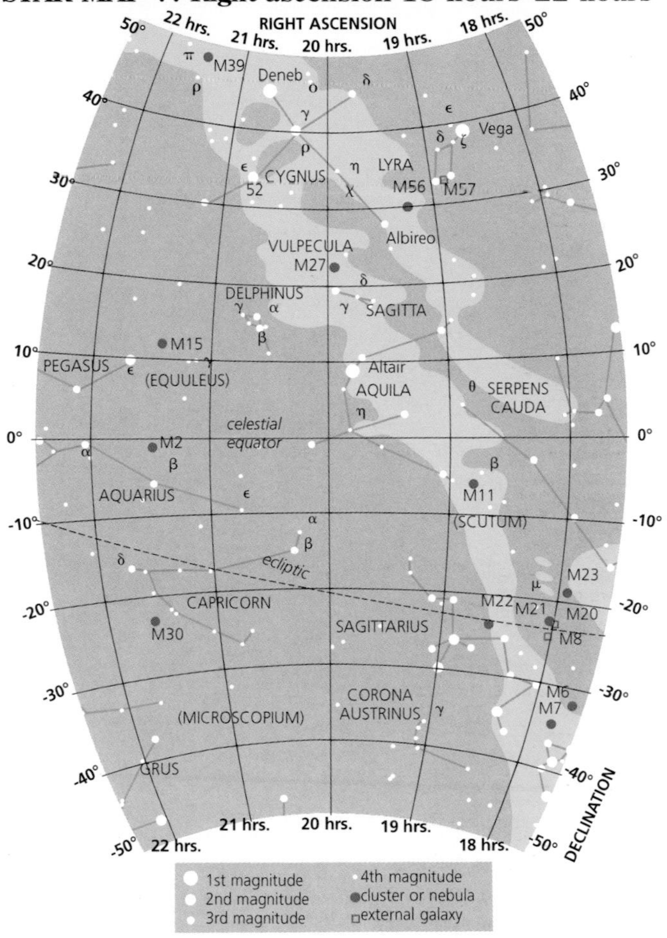

STAR MAP 8: Southern circumpolar stars

▲ **The Milky Way** is a fabulous sight among the circumpolar stars.

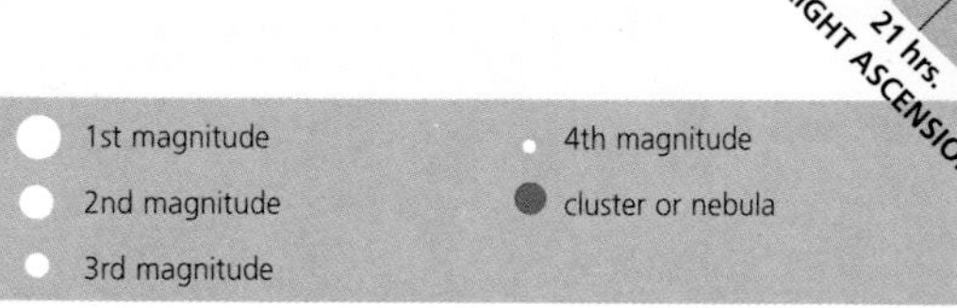

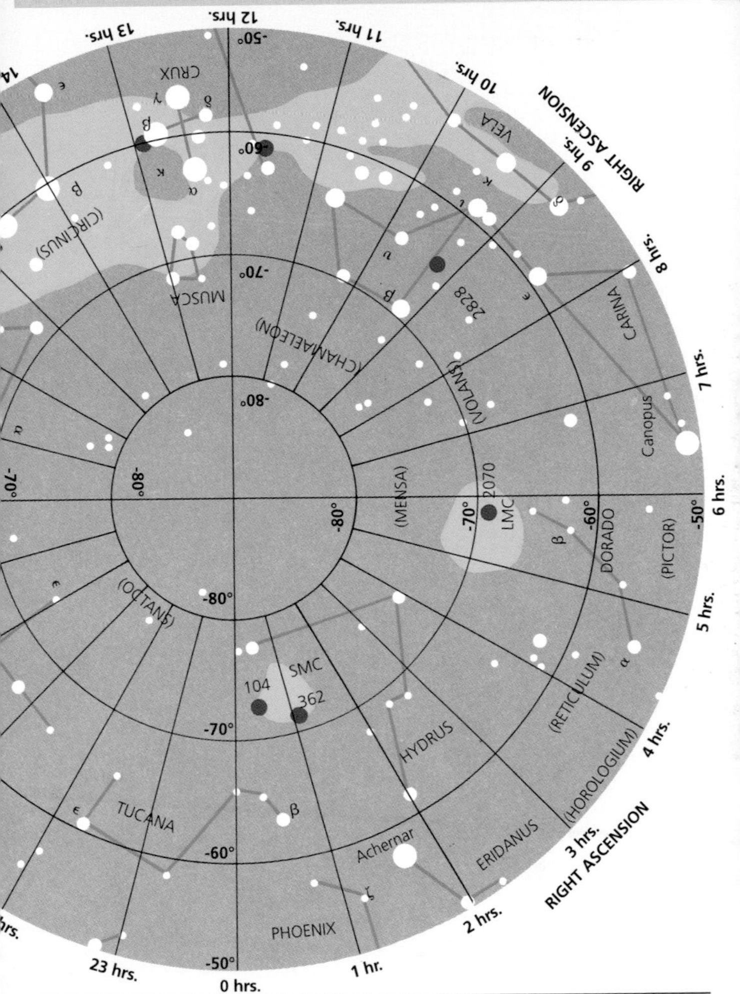
CRUX
MUSCA
(CIRCINUS)
(CHAMAELEON)
VELA
CARINA
(VOLANS)
Canopus
(MENSA)
LMC
2070
2828
DORADO
(PICTOR)
(RETICULUM)
(HOROLOGIUM)
HYDRUS
ERIDANUS
Achernar
PHOENIX
TUCANA
(OCTANS)
SMC
104
362
RIGHT ASCENSION
0 hrs.
1 hr.
2 hrs.
3 hrs.
4 hrs.
5 hrs.
6 hrs.
7 hrs.
8 hrs.
9 hrs.
10 hrs.
11 hrs.
12 hrs.
13 hrs.
23 hrs.
-50°
-60°
-70°
-80°

Observation notes on the constellations

All the stars and other objects that have been mentioned in these notes can be found on the star maps and should be visible with binoculars—although the nebulae and clusters will look much more impressive if a powerful telescope is available.

Andromeda (And, star map 2)
This large constellation contains the famous Andromeda Galaxy, M31, which can be easily seen with the naked eye in a dark sky; binoculars show a small, hazy companion, M32, both around two million light-years away. α (Alpheratz): RA 6 hrs. 6 mins., dec +29°, mag 2·0.

▼ **The globular cluster** M2 in Aquarius is one of the most remote objects in our galaxy to be visible with binoculars.

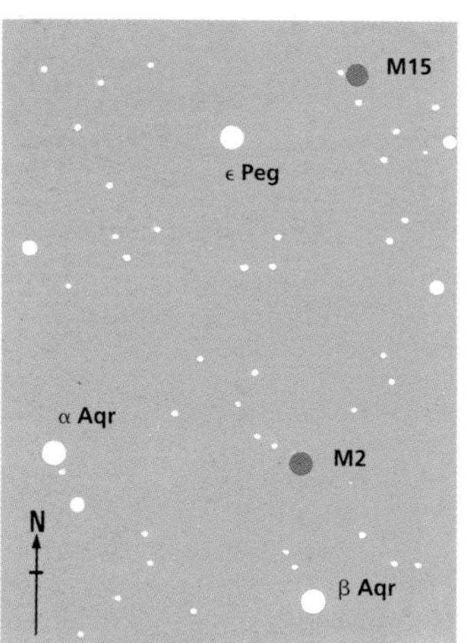

Apus, the Bird of Paradise
(Aps, star map 8)
A very faint group near the South Pole. α: RA 14 hrs. 42 mins., dec –79°, mag 3·8.

Aquarius, the Water Bearer
(Aqr, star maps 2 and 7)
This zodiacal constellation only contains two bright stars, but the little group of faint stars around ζ has a distinctive shape. Use the special chart to locate the globular cluster M2, which appears with binoculars as a very small, hazy spot (diameter around 100 light-years; distance 55,000 light-years). The mag 4 star τ is a wide binocular double. α (Sadalmelik): RA 22 hrs. 3 mins., dec -0.5°, mag 2·9—one of the closest bright stars to the celestial equator.

Aquila, the Eagle
(Aql, star map 7)
A notable Milky Way group whose brightest star, Altair, is one of the Sun's closest neighbors, only 16 light-years away. η Aql is a bright Cepheid (see page 52); fine star fields close to δ, α (Altair): RA 19 hrs. 48 mins., dec +8.5°, mag 0·8.

Ara, the Altar
(Ara, star map 8)
A conspicuous, compact group in the southern Milky Way. β: RA 17 hrs. 21 mins., dec –55.5°, mag 2·8.

Aries, the Ram
(Ari, star map 3)
A small and rather faint group but noticeable because there are few stars nearby. α (Hamal): RA 2 hrs. 4 mins., dec +23°, mag 2·0.

▲ An amateur photograph of Auriga, showing the stars as trails. The brightest star is Capella.

Auriga, the Charioteer
(Aur, star map 3)
This is a magnificent constellation lying in a faint part of the northern Milky Way. Its three prominent open clusters, M36, M37, and M38, are all fine binocular objects—M37 is the largest. Theta is a challenging object for a 100-millimeter telescope (mags 2·6 and 7·1, separated by only 3·6"). ϵ is a very unusual dark-eclipsing variable star (see page 51) with a period of 27 years; the next minimum will occur in the year 2010. α (Capella): RA 5 hrs. 13 mins.; dec +46°, mag 0·1.

Boötes, the Herdsman
(Boo, star map 6)
A prominent, kite-shaped group, with the bright reddish Arcturus in its "tail." δ has a mag 9 companion almost 2' to the east, but there are few deep-sky objects. α (Arcturus): RA 14 hrs. 13 mins., dec +19.5°, mag -0·1.

Cancer, the Crab
(Cnc, star map 4)
A faint zodiacal group, interesting for the bright cluster Praesepe (M44), which looks like a large, hazy patch with the naked eye. M44 must be much older than the Pleiades in Taurus because it does not contain luminous white stars; they are all yellowish main-sequence dwarfs or red giants. This group is around 15 light-years across and 500 light-years away. M67 is older, and with binoculars it appears as a misty spot. β: RA 8 hrs. 14 mins., dec +9.5°, mag 3·5.

Canis Major, the Greater Dog
(CMa, star map 4)
A bright Milky Way group, containing the brightest star in the sky, Sirius. Viewed from north European latitudes Sirius never rises very high above the southern horizon, usually twinkling violently through the unsteady atmosphere. The open cluster M41 is easy to locate with binoculars, α (Sirius): RA 6 hrs. 43 mins., dec -16.5°, mag -1·5.

Canis Minor, the Lesser Dog
(CMi, star map 4)
Only its leading star is obvious; like Sirius, it is a binary with a white dwarf companion. α (Procyon): RA 7 hrs. 37 mins., dec, +5.5°, mag 0·3.

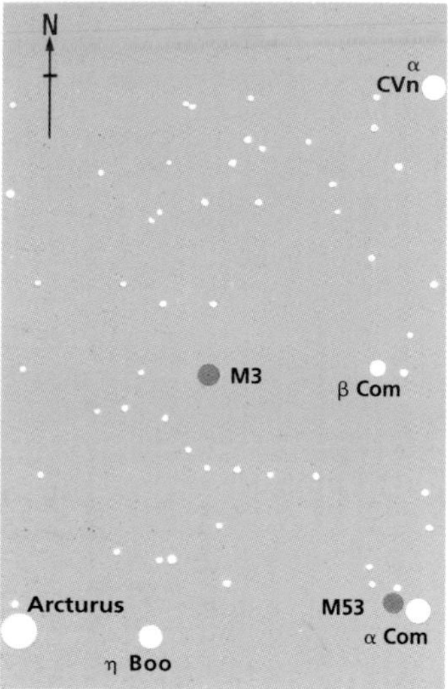

▲ **M3**, in Canes Venatici, is one of the finest globular clusters in the sky and appears with binoculars as a hazy patch on a line from α CVn toward Arcturus in Boötes.

Canes Venatici, the Hunting Dogs
(CVn, star map 5)
Only the leading star is obvious, lying south of Ursa Major. Use the accompanying chart to locate M3, one of the finest globular clusters. The external galaxy M51 may also be glimpsed as a very faint, hazy disk. α (Cor Caroli): RA 12 hrs. 54 mins., dec +38.5°, mag 2·8.

Capricorn, the Sea Goat
(Cap, star map 7)
A large but faint zodiacal constellation, containing the wide, naked-eye double star α (mags 3·6 and 4·3, 6' 16" apart) and an easy binocular double, β, which has a mag 6 companion 3' 25" away. The globular cluster M30 is a difficult binocular object from high northern latitudes. α (Dabih): RA 20 hrs. 18 mins., dec -15°, mag 3·0.

Carina, the Keel
(Car, star map 8)
A large and brilliant southern constellation containing several bright star clusters and groups, including the globular cluster NGC 2808, visible with binoculars. Magnificent sweeping in the Milky Way close to Vela, α (Canopus): RA 6 hrs. 23 mins., dec -52.5°, mag -0·7.

Cassiopeia
(Cas, star map 1)
A small but unmistakable constellation, its five brightest stars forming a conspicuous "M" or "W" near the north celestial pole. γ is an unusual variable, which suddenly brightened to mag 1·7 from its usual 2·4 in 1938. ρ, usually mag 5, sometimes fades to 6. There are rich Milky Way fields; note particularly the clusters M52 and NGC 663. α (Shedir): RA O hrs. 38 mins., dec +56.5°, mag 2·2.

Centaurus, the Centaur
(Cen, star maps 5, 6, and 8)
An extensive constellation, α is a bright binary star, although it cannot be resolved without an adequate telescope. Known as Rigil Kentaurus, it is the closest naked-eye star to the Sun. Centaurus contains the closest and brightest globular cluster in the sky, labeled ω. Binoculars show it as an immense hazy patch around two thirds the Moon's diameter. α (Rigil Kentaurus): RA 14 hrs. 36 mins., dec -60.5°, mag 0·1.

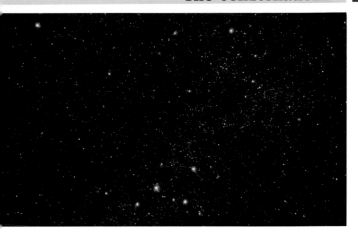

▲ **The "W" shape** of Cassiopeia stands out at center bottom. Polaris in Ursa Minor is the bright star at top left.

Cepheus

(Cep, star map 1)
Not easy to identify, but it contains interesting objects. μ was called the Garnet Star by Herschel due to its red wine color; it is slightly variable. δ is the prototype Cepheid (see page 53 and use the chart there to observe its changes). It has a mag 5 companion 41" away. α (Alderamin): RA 21 hrs. 17 mins. dec +62.5°, mag 2·4.

Cetus, the Whale

(Cet, star maps 2 and 3)
An extensive, faint constellation, although the little triangle of α, γ, and δ is fairly obvious. Mira, or *o*, is a long-period variable (mentioned on page 52), ranging from around mag 10 at its minimum to as bright as mag 2 (but

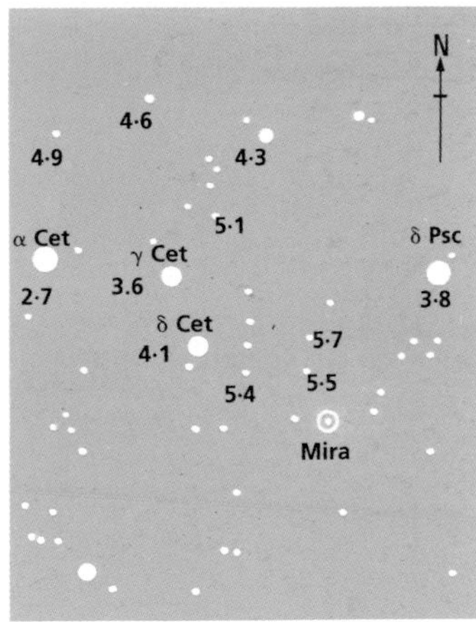

▲ **If the long-period** variable Mira (*o* Ceti) is above magnitude 6, it can be located with this chart and followed as it brightens or fades.

usually around mag 4) at maximum, in a period of around eleven months. The next observable maxima should occur during mid-March 2006, early-February 2007, and early-January 2008.

Coma Berenices, Berenices' Hair
(Com, star map 5)
Although containing no star brighter than mag 4, Coma can be distinguished as a faint scattering of stars in an otherwise dull patch of sky. It contains one of the largest known clusters of galaxies—several thousand of them—but only a few are prominent. The chart shows the positions of two that are only visible with binoculars (M64 and M85); M53 is brighter than either, but it is a globular cluster. Both galaxies are around 40 million light-years away. α: RA 13 hrs. 8 mins., dec +18°, mag 4·2.

The adjacent regions of Leo and Virgo also contain numerous galaxies, and these are all part of the Local Supercluster, which spreads across 100 million light-years of space.

▼ **Some of the brighter** galaxies in the Coma Virgo region, together with the globular cluster M53, the easiest Messier object shown here.

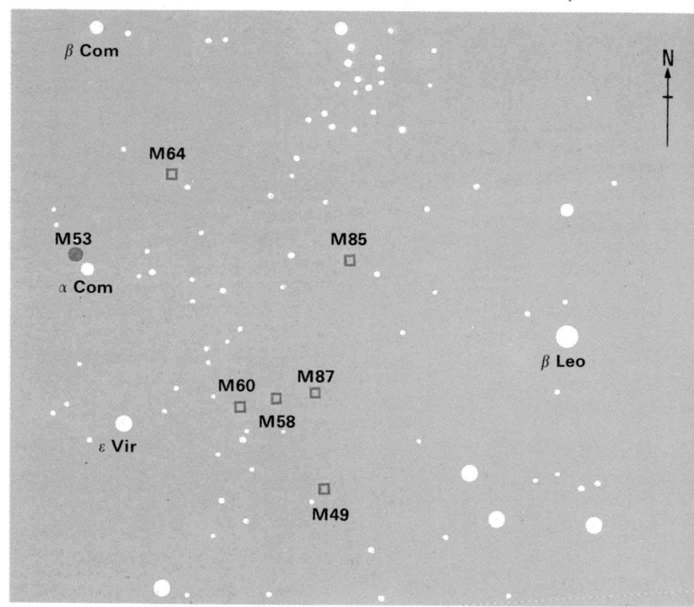

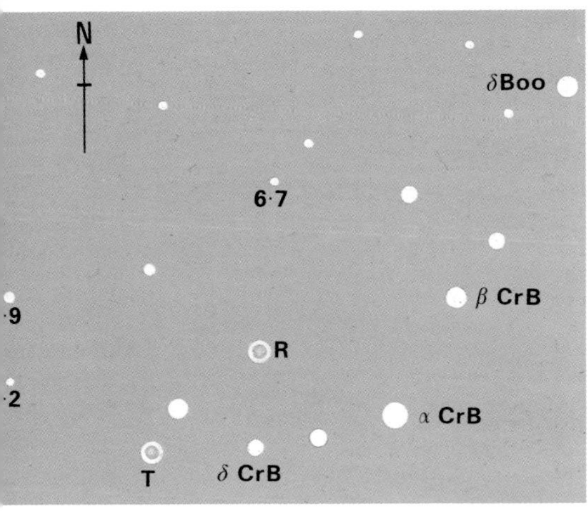

◀ **A chart** for the unusual variables R and T Coronae Borealis.

Corona Borealis, the Northern Crown
(CrB, star map 6)
Although it is small, this group is easily identified from its semicircular outline. Note variable R, normally mag 6, which, at unpredictable intervals, sinks in a few days to as faint as mag 14; see the chart above. T rose to brief, naked-eye visibility in 1866 and 1946. α (Alphecca): RA 15 hrs. 33 mins., dec +27°, mag 2·3.

Crux, the Cross
(Crx, star map 8)
The smallest constellation in the sky but one of the most famous. It contains one of the finest double stars, α (Acrux), mags 1·4 and 1·9, separation 4·4". Its position is RA 12 hrs. 24 mins., dec -63°.

Cygnus, the Swan
(Cyg, star map 7)
One of the finest northern constellations, the Milky Way around γ is very rich and contains the bright cluster M39. The stars are too scattered for the best effect. *o* is one of the best binocular pairs, the mag 4 yellow star making the mag 5 companion look blue. β (mags 3 and 5·5, separation 34") may be divided. Note the long-period variable χ, which reaches mag 4·5 at its maximum and can be identified by its red color. Period is around 406 days. α (Deneb): RA 20 hrs. 40 mins., dec +45°, mag 1·3.

Delphinus, the Dolphin
(Del, star map 7)
A small, distinct constellation close to a bright section of the Milky Way. In 1967 a naked-eye nova was discovered within its boundaries. γ is a beautiful double, mags 4 and 5, separation 10". RA 20 hrs. 38 mins., dec +15°, mag 3·8.

Dorado, the Dolphin
(Dor, star map 8)
A far southern constellation, interesting mostly because it contains one of our galaxy's satellites, the Large Magellanic Cloud, around 160,000 light-years away and looking like a large, hazy patch. This contains many superb objects, including NGC 2070, a naked-eye emission nebula. β is a bright Cepheid (see page 52).
α: RA 4 hrs. 33 mins., dec -55°, mag 3·3.

Draco, the Dragon
(Dra, star map 1)
This is a winding constellation, extending around a large arc of the northern sky. The two stars β and γ are the easiest to identify. Nearby is υ, a very attractive pair of mag 5 stars around 1' apart. α (Thuban): RA 14 hrs. 3 mins., dec +64.5°, mag 3·6.

Equuleus, the Little Horse
(Equ, star map 7)
This tiny constellation only contains three obvious stars. One of them, γ, is an attractive wide double, mags 4·5 and 6. α: RA 21 hrs. 13 mins., dec +5°, mag 3·9.

Eridanus
(Eri, star maps 3 and 8)
A winding constellation extending from the far southern sky to equatorial latitudes. Note the reddish tint of γ—a red giant star. α (Achernar): RA 1 hr. 36 mins., dec -57.5°, mag 0·5.

Gemini, the Twins (Gem, star map 4)
One of the most interesting of all the constellations. It lies on the most northern part of the ecliptic, and the Sun moves into it from adjacent Taurus on the first day of the northern summer. At this time it is

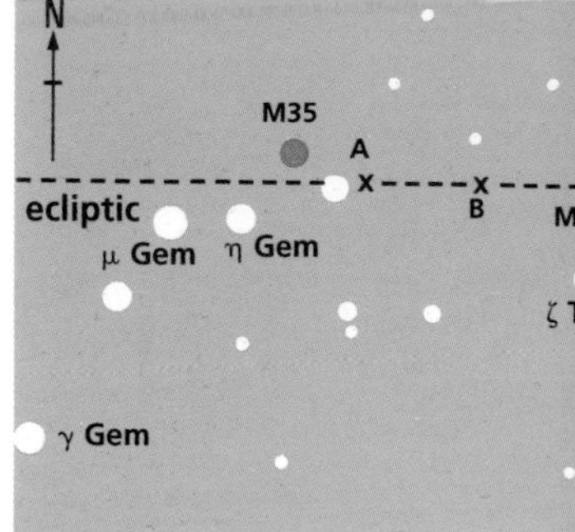

▲ **In Gemini** A is the Sun's position in northern midsummer, B is where Uranus was found in 1781.

only one degree or so away from the bright open cluster M35. This is also the point where Herschel discovered the planet Uranus in 1781. μ and η both have lovely golden tints, while ε and ζ have faint binocular companions—the latter being the more impressive. β (Pollux): RA 7 hrs. 42 mins., dec +28°, mag 1·1.

Hercules
(Her, star map 6)
Not obvious until the quadrilateral or "keystone" of π, η, ζ, and ε is identified but a constellation for the double-star enthusiast with an adequate telescope. M13 is its most famous object: one of the brightest globular clusters in the sky and just visible with the naked eye. It is around 25,000 light-years away and may contain half a million stars. M92, another globular, is harder to find because there are no nearby bright stars as guides; it is half as far away as M13. α (Rasalgethi): RA 17 hrs. 12 mins., dec +1°, mag 3·5.

Hydra, the Water Serpent

(Hya, star maps 4 and 5)
A faint, rambling group; only Alphard and the little collection of stars south of Cancer, marking its head, are obvious. α (Alphard): RA 9 hrs. 25 mins. dec -8.5°, mag 2·0.

Leo, the Lion

(Leo, star map 5)
A zodiacal constellation, α lying within one degree of the ecliptic, so that both the Moon and the planets can occult it. Leo lies close to the huge groups of galaxies in Coma and Virgo, and at least two objects, M65 and M66, are just detectable with binoculars if the sky is dark; use the accompanying chart to locate them. α (Regulus): RA 10 hrs. 6 mins., dec +12°, mag 1·4.

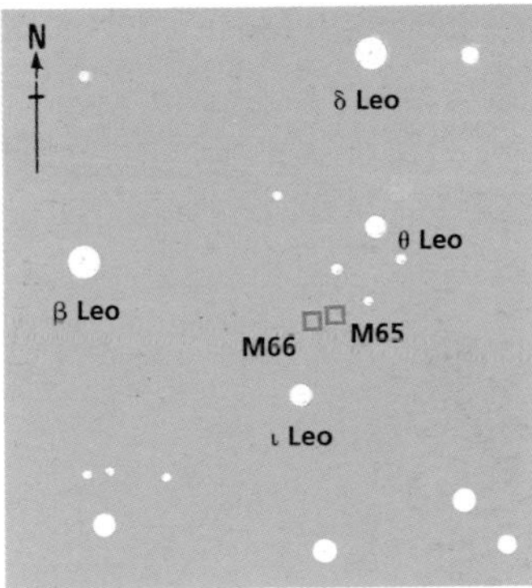

▲ **The pair** of spiral galaxies in Leo, M65 and M66.

Lepus, the Hare

(Lep, star map 3)
A small but conspicuous group south of Orion. γ is a very fine binocular double (mags 4 and 6·5, separation 1.5'), while the globular cluster M79 can be seen as a hazy spot. α (Arneb): RA 5 hrs. 31 mins., dec -18°, mag 2·6.

Libra, the Scales

(Lib, star map 6)
A large zodiacal constellation, but only α and β are obvious. α has a wide mag 6 companion. α (Zubenelgenubi): RA 14 hrs. 48 mins., dec -16°, mag 2·8.

Lupus, the Wolf

(Lup, star map 6)
A small, prominent constellation in a rich part of the southern Milky Way. η is a mag 4 star with a mag 9 companion 2' away, and NGC 5822 is a bright open cluster. α: RA 14 hrs. 39 mins., dec -47°, mag 2·3.

◀ **Dense star field** close to γ Cygni.

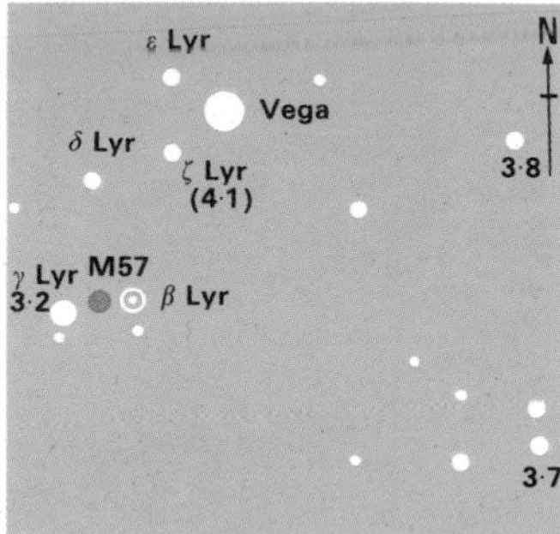

▲ **A chart** for the eclipsing star β Lyrae, also showing the position of M57, the Ring Nebula.

Lyra, the Lyre

(Lyr, star map 7)

A small but interesting group. ε can be separated by the naked eye; ζ (mag 4) has a mag 6 companion 44' away. δ is another naked-eye pair. β is an eclipsing binary (see page 51): it is almost as bright as its neighbor when it is at its brightest, but a magnitude dimmer when it passes through an eclipse. M57, the Ring Nebula, is barely detectable with binoculars; M56 is a faint globular, α (Vega): RA 18 hrs. 35 mins., dec +38.5°, mag 0·0.

Monoceros, the Unicorn

(Mon, star map 4)

Most of the stars in this group are faint, but the Milky Way is magnificent. The cluster NGC 2244 can be seen with the naked eye. M50 and NGC 2506 are other fine clusters. M50 is so compact that it appears as a hazy patch when it is viewed with binoculars. α: RA 7 hrs. 39 mins., dec -9.5°, mag 3·9.

Ophiuchus, the Serpent Bearer

(Oph, star map 6)

Although not one of the twelve zodiacal constellations, the ecliptic passes through it. Superb Milky Way star fields are to the south; M10 and M12 are bright globular clusters, while M9, M19, and M62 are fainter globulars. The whole region is worth sweeping on a clear night. An obvious binocular group of 8th magnitude stars around one degree away from β was not, strangely enough, included in the early catalogs of deep-sky objects. α (Rasalhague): RA 17 hrs. 33 mins., dec +12.5°, mag 2·1.

▼ **The constellation** Lyra with its bright star, Vega.

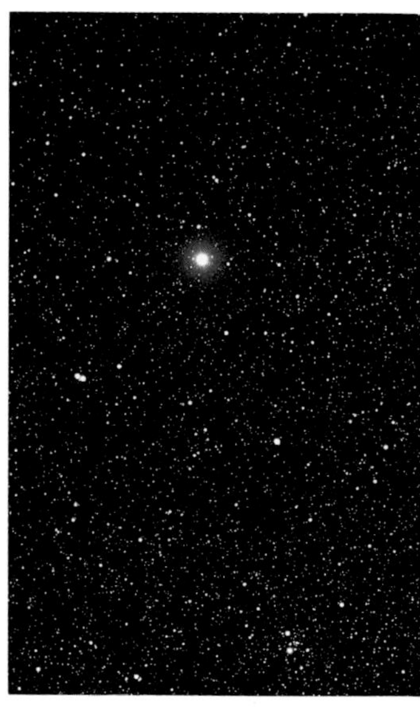

Orion

(Ori, star map 3)
This bright constellation contains no less than seven 1st magnitude stars—more than any other group. All, apart from Betelgeuse, form a true association in space, being hot young stars. Rigel (β) is one of the most luminous known stars in our galaxy, at 50,000 times as bright as the Sun. δ is a difficult binocular double, with a mag 6·5 companion to the north 53" away. The famous Great Nebula, M42, shows many irregularities due to dark nebulae. β (Rigel): RA 5 hrs. 12 mins. dec -8.5°, mag 0·1.

Pavo, the Peacock

(Pav, star map 8)
This group contains two interesting stars: κ, a Cepheid (mag 3·9–4·9, period 9·1 days), and an irregular variable, λ (mag 3·5–4·5). NGC 6752 is a huge globular cluster, more than half the Moon's diameter across. α: RA 20 hrs. 22 mins.; dec –57°, mag 1·9.

Pegasus

(Peg, star maps 2 and 7)
The Great Square is easy to see once it is located, but it is not always easy to find at first, because it looks larger in the sky than on a map. ϵ is an easy binocular double (mags 2·5 and 8·5, separation of almost 2') that acts as a guide to the globular cluster, M15, easily seen in binoculars. α (Markab): RA 23 hrs. 2 mins., dec +15°, mag 2·5.

Perseus

(Per, star maps 1 and 3)
A magnificent constellation in the northern Milky Way. Its most famous object is the eclipsing binary β (Algol), described on page 51. NGC 869 and 884 form the Double Cluster, visible with the naked eye and a fine binocular object. M34, a more scattered cluster, can also be seen with the naked eye. α (Mirfak): RA 3 hrs. 21 mins., dec +50°, mag 1·8.

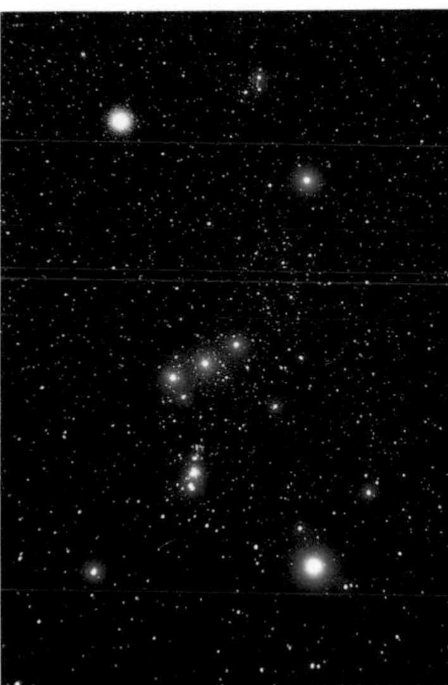

▲ **The three "belt"** stars of Orion, with the Great Nebula, M42, to the south.

Pisces, the Fish

(Psc, star map 2)
A faint zodiacal group, containing the vernal equinox—the point where the Sun crosses the celestial equator at the start of the northern spring. Due to the slow gyration of Earth's axis, the vernal equinox was in the adjacent Aries constellation two millennia ago. α (Katain): RA 1 hr. 59 mins., dec +2.5°, mag 3·8.

▲ **The Double Cluster** in Perseus is found in a rich region of the Milky Way.

Piscis Austrinus, the Southern Fish
(PsA, star map 2)
A small group marked by its leader Fomalhaut, which shines in an empty part of the sky. α (Fomalhaut): RA 22 hrs. 55 mins., dec -30°, mag 1·2.

Puppis
(Pup, star map 4)
This small, bright group contains many open clusters and fine Milky Way star fields. Note particularly M47—a magnificent loose group that is almost equal to the Moon's diameter, and M93. M46 is faint for binocular observation. ζ: RA 8 hrs. 2 mins., dec –40°, mag 2·3.

Sagitta, the Arrow
(Sge, star map 7)
A small but distinctive group lying in the Milky Way. Look slightly south of the midway point between γ and δ for M71 (see the chart on page 90). Appearing as a dim, hazy spot, it is either a very compressed open cluster or an extremely unusual globular. γ: RA 19 hrs. 57 mins., dec +19°, mag 3·5.

Sagittarius, the Archer
(Sgr, star map 7)
An amazing zodiacal constellation lying in the densest part of the Milky Way—the region toward the center of our galaxy. Clusters and nebulae are strewn so thickly that no guide to interesting objects is really necessary, and the ones shown on the map are only a few of the more obvious ones. M8, the Lagoon Nebula, is a bright cluster enveloped in haze, while M20 is the Trifid Nebula—a prominent, irregular patch next to the open cluster M21. M23 is another bright cluster, while M22 is a super globular. The constellation contains 15 Messier objects altogether, but most are difficult to see from high northern latitudes. ϵ (Kaus Australis): RA 18 hrs. 21 mins., dec -34.5°, mag 1·8.

Scorpius, the Scorpion
(Sco, star map 6)
After Orion, it is perhaps the brightest constellation, with red Antares in its head and a curved "stinger." Like its neighbor Sagittarius, Scorpius contains the densest part of the Milky Way, and clusters and nebulae abound, but there are also some interesting stars. The red supergiant Antares is as large as the orbit of Mars and slightly variable. ν is an attractive binocular double, mags 4·5 and 6·5, separation 41". M4 and M80 are both globular clusters, M4 is the larger of the two and lies in the

► **The Trifid Nebula** is around 2,300 light-years from the Sun. The lanes are due to huge, dark interstellar clouds between us and the nebula.

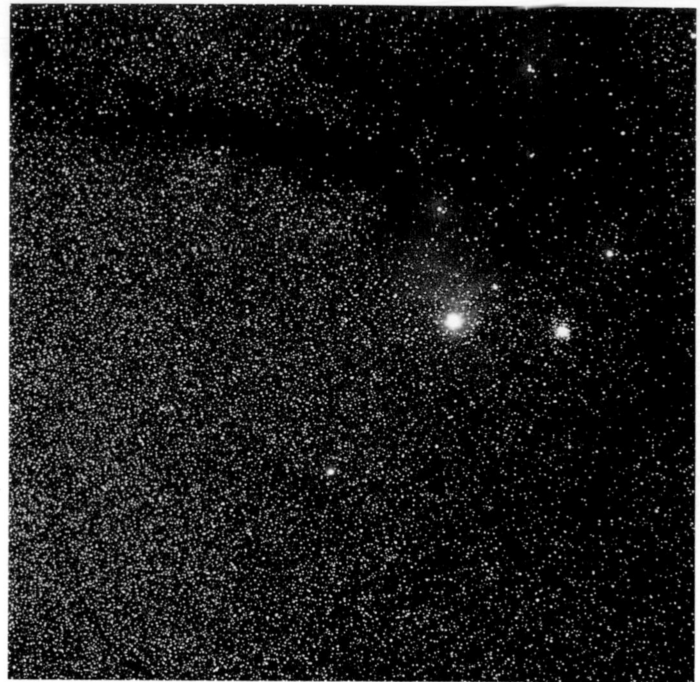

same binocular field as Antares itself. The open clusters M6 and M7 are among the finest. α (Antares): RA 16 hrs. 26 mins., dec -26.5°, mag around 1·1 (variable).

Scutum, the Shield

(Sct, star map 6)

A faint but distinctive group in a superb region of the Milky Way, containing the superb open cluster M11. α: RA 18 hrs. 32 mins., dec -8.5°, mag 3·8.

Serpens, the Serpent

(Ser, star map 6)

This constellation represents a snake being held by Ophiuchus and is divided into a head (Caput) and a body (Cauda). It contains M5 (see chart on opposite page)—one of the largest and brightest globular clusters. δ is a fine double star (mags 4·2 and 5·2, separation 44"). α (Unukalhai): RA 15 hrs. 42 mins., dec +6.5°, mag 2·7.

◀ **Red Antares** in Scorpius is a giant star that is around 500 light-years away; it is around 10,000 times as luminous as the Sun.

Taurus, the Bull

(Tau, star map 3)
A prominent zodiacal group with more than its fair share of interesting objects. The bright, very scattered Hyades cluster, to the west of Aldebaran, looks like a sprinkle of colored jewels through binoculars. The Pleiades, three times as distant at around 400 light-years, are much more compact and contain very luminous white stars of a type that has burned out and disappeared in the much older Hyades. At its distance of only 65 light-years, Aldebaran is twice as close as the Hyades. τ is an attractive binocular double, mags 4·5 and 8·5, distance 1'. The planetary M1 can barely be spotted, around 1° NW of ζ; this is the Crab Nebula—the remains of the supernova of 1054, α (Aldebaran): RA 4 hrs. 33 mins., dec +16.5°, mag 0·9.

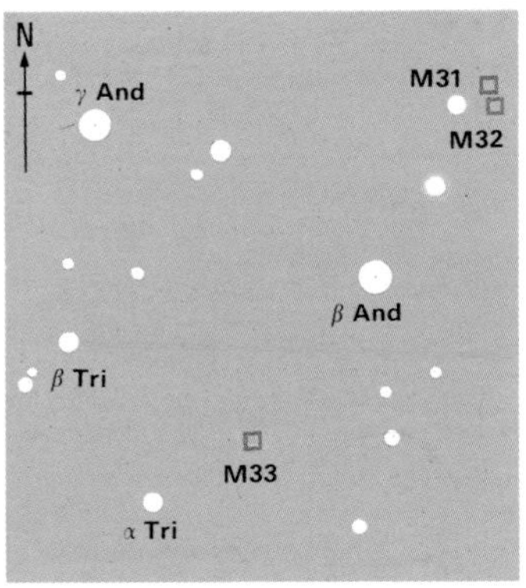

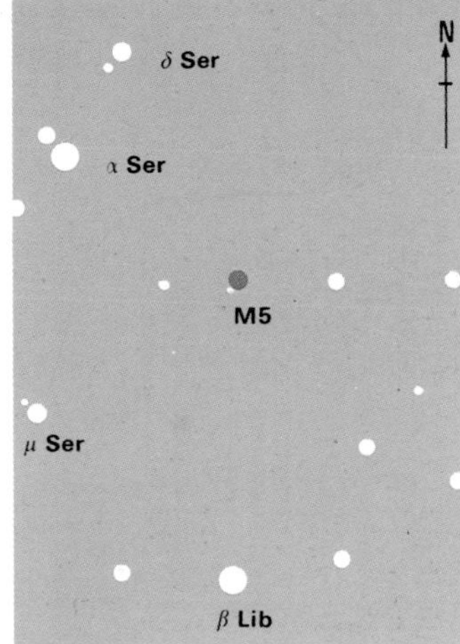

▲ **M5 in Serpens** rivals the Great Cluster in Hercules for brightness. It is 27,000 light-years away from Earth.

Triangulum, the Triangle

(Tri, star map 2)
A small but distinct group containing the interesting galaxy M33. At least as large as the Moon, it is incredibly faint and difficult to see: a real challenge even on the clearest nights. Excellent dark adaptation is essential. Slowly pass the binoculars over the area and use averted vision, which means directing the gaze away from the region so that the image falls on the more sensitive margin of the retina. Slightly farther off than M31, it is a much smaller object, with around 1/40th of its mass. β: RA 2 hrs. 7 mins., dec +35°, mag 3·0.

◀ **Elusive M33**, in Triangulum, can just be detected with binoculars in a transparent sky.

Triangulum Australe, the Southern Triangle
(TrA, star map 8)
A small, high southern group on the edge of the Milky Way. NGC 6025 is a fine open cluster. α: RA 16 hrs. 43 mins., dec -69°, mag 1·9.

Tucana, the Toucan
(Tuc, star map 8)
Containing the Small Magellanic Cloud, this constellation also includes the bright globular cluster 47 (NGC 104), which rivals ω Cen. β may be too difficult for binoculars: mags both 4·5, separation 27". NGC 362 is another fine globular. α: RA 22 hrs. 15 mins., dec -60.5°, mag 2·8.

Ursa Major, the Great Bear
(UMa, star maps 1 and 5)
Often called the Big Dipper or the Plow, the outline of this constellation is known to most people, although it extends far beyond the seven bright stars. ζ (Mizar) is mentioned on page 50. The faint planetary cluster M97 may be spotted with binoculars in a very dark sky. α (Dubhe): RA 11 hrs. 1 min., dec +62°, mag 1·8.

Ursa Minor, the Little Bear
(UMi, star map 1)
The north polar constellation, containing the North Star or Polaris. α (Polaris): RA 2 hrs. 15 mins., dec +89°, mag 2·0.

Vela, the Sails
(Vel, star maps 4 and 8)
A bright Milky Way group. γ is a testing double (mags 1·8 and 4·2, distance 42 "), just visible with good binoculars. The nearby cluster NGC 2547 can be seen with the naked eye. γ: RA 8 hrs. 8 mins., dec -47°, mag 1·7.

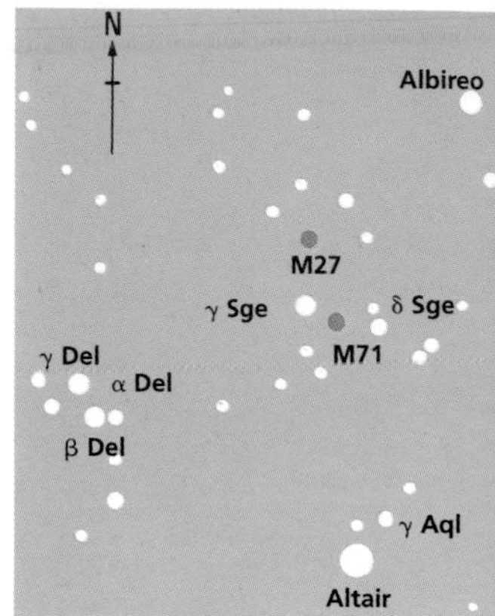

Virgo, the Virgin
(Vir, star map 5)
A large zodiacal constellation, best known for the galaxies within its confines—although few are visible with binoculars. The chart on page 80 shows the positions of the brightest (M49, M58, and M87), as well as the fainter M60. α (Spica): RA 13 hrs. 23 mins., dec -11°, mag 1·0.

Vulpecula, the Fox
(Vul, star map 7) This is a very small Milky Way group, but it contains M27—one of the largest and brightest planetary nebulae in the sky (see chart). α: RA 19 hrs. 27 mins., dec +24.5°, mag 4·4.

▶ **The large** planetary M27, the Dumbbell Nebula, is a bright binocular object but difficult to see in the faint stars of Vulpecula—(see chart above). M71 in Sagitta is also shown.

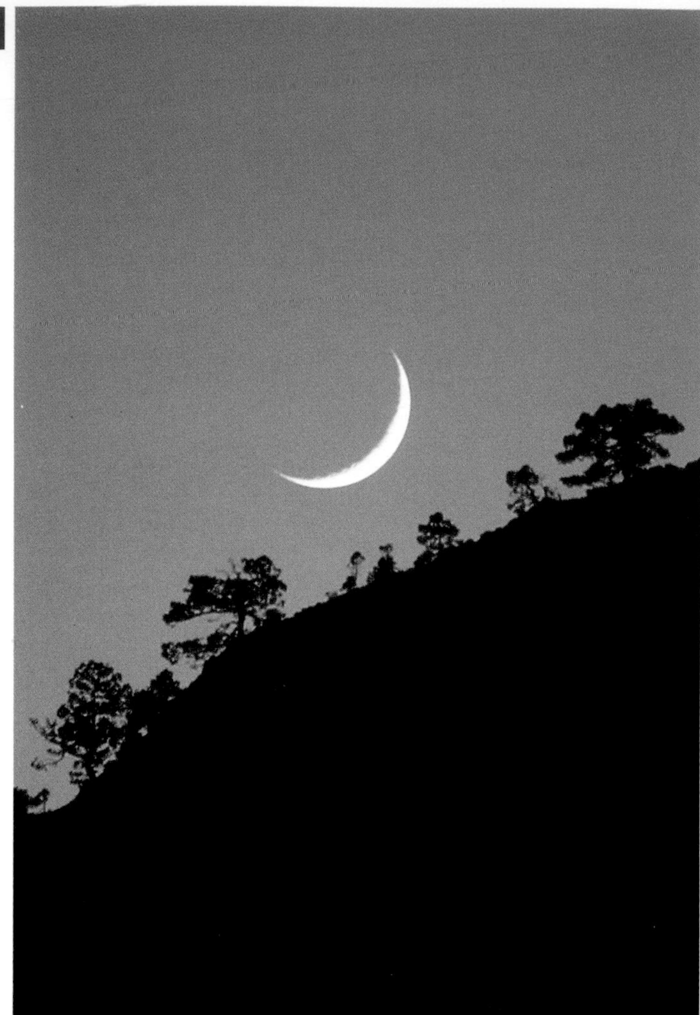

The Moon

Of all the objects in the sky, the Moon is the one that appears to undergo the most dramatic changes, since it passes through a complete cycle of phases once every month. This change, though, is only of movement and light. The lunar surface is inert, airless, and dead; the last dramatic events happened there around three billion years ago, and they are still recorded, apparently fresh, on its crater-pocked face.

The Moon passes through phases because it only shines by reflecting sunlight. The Moon, like Earth, is always half-lit by the Sun. As it goes through its phases each night, different features of its surface are illuminated. A lot of detail can be seen with a small telescope or binoculars, so it is not surprising that the Moon is a favorite object for anyone with astronomy as a hobby.

The Moon's cycle

It takes the Moon 29.5 days to pass through its phases, and this is known as the lunar month. During this time the sunrise and sunset line, or *terminator*, slowly passes across the Earth-turned hemisphere: sunrise before a full Moon, sunset after a full Moon.

At a new Moon the dark hemisphere faces Earth and cannot be seen, since it is very close to the Sun in the sky. After two or three days it has moved far enough east to be seen as a thin crescent in the

▼ **The Moon** shows phases because the Sun can only illuminate one hemisphere. It rotates once on its axis during the lunar month, therefore always keeping the same face toward Earth.

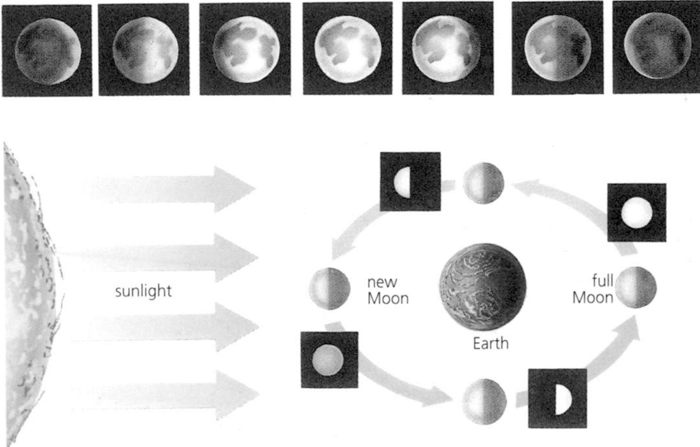

evening sky; after seven days it forms a perfect half—known as first quarter—lying around 90° away from the Sun.

The following week sees it in the *gibbous* state, until at full Moon it is situated across from the Sun in the sky, rising at sunset. After this the phases pass in the reverse order, the Moon rising later and later in the night, until it disappears in the dawn sky.

Unless the lineup between the three bodies is perfect and an eclipse occurs, the Moon is invisible at new Moon since it is hidden in the Sun's glare. It is interesting to try to spot the thin crescent setting in the west a couple of days after a new Moon or rising in the east a couple of days before a new Moon. Binoculars will be helpful in locating the thin line of light, perhaps with the complete dark side faintly lit by reflected light from Earth.

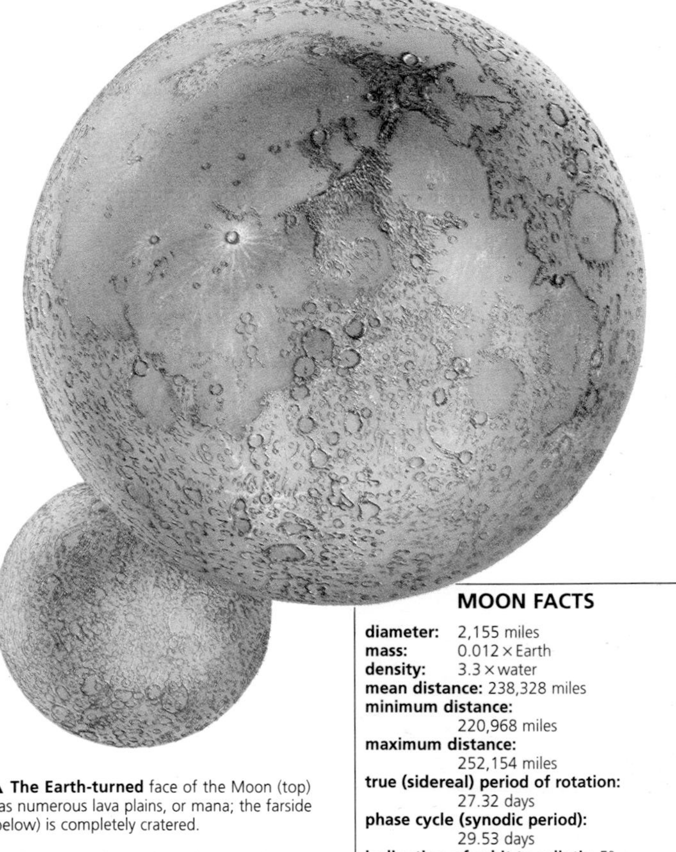

▲ **The Earth-turned** face of the Moon (top) ıas numerous lava plains, or mana; the farside below) is completely cratered.

◀ **The Moon** shows phases because the Sun an only illuminate one hemisphere. It rotates ›nce on its axis during the lunar month, therefore ılways keeping the same face toward Earth.

MOON FACTS

diameter: 2,155 miles
mass: 0.012 × Earth
density: 3.3 × water
mean distance: 238,328 miles
minimum distance: 220,968 miles
maximum distance: 252,154 miles
true (sidereal) period of rotation: 27.32 days
phase cycle (synodic period): 29.53 days
inclination of orbit to ecliptic: 5°
axial inclination: 6.5°
angular diameter: 29' 21" (min.); 33' 30" (max.)

Lunar eclipses

If the Moon moved precisely along the ecliptic (which could only happen if it revolved exactly in the plane of Earth's orbit), the lineup with the Sun at new and full Moon would be perfect, and there would always be an eclipse of the Sun and the Moon respectively at these times.

However, the Moon's orbit is inclined at 5° to the ecliptic, so eclipses are relatively rare. A lunar eclipse occurs when the Moon passes into Earth's shadow. At a total eclipse it completely passes into the central shadow, or umbra. An eclipse may last for several hours and may be total for more than an hour. But even when it is totally eclipsed, the Moon is always dimly visible because Earth's atmosphere passes some light into the shadow, giving it a reddish-brown color.

▼ **An eclipse** of the Moon occurs when it passes through the long shadow cast by Earth.

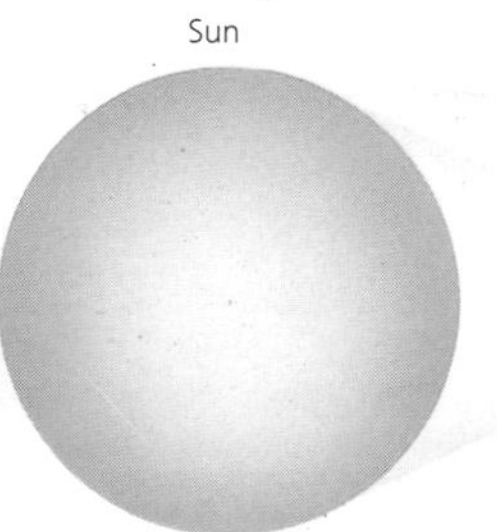

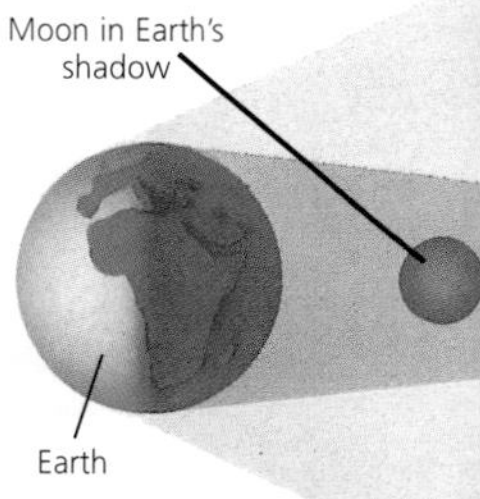

LUNAR ECLIPSE TABLE			
date	**type**	**max. time (hrs., mins.)**	**area of visibility**
2006 September 7	partial	1 h 33 m	Europe, Africa, Asia, Australia
2007 March 3	total	1 h 14 m	Americas, Europe, Africa, Asia
2007 August 28	total	1 h 31 m	east Asia, Australia, Pacific, Americas
2008 February 21	total	51 m	Pacific, Americas, Europe, Africa
2008 August 16	partial	3 h 9 m	South America, Europe, Afr., Asia, Aust.
2009 December 31	partial	1 h 2 m	Europe, Africa, Asia, Australia

▲ **Total eclipse of the Moon.** The Moon in the progress of a lunar eclipse. It can take up to six hours for the Moon to completely pass through Earth's shadow, and the totality of the eclipse can last for 1.75 hours.

Total eclipses are especially interesting, because some are much darker than others. This is due to the varying transparency of the atmosphere. Partial eclipses, on the other hand, are of little interest, since the dazzling, uneclipsed portion of the surface blots out the delicate shadow coloring. The eclipse on December 30, 1982, was so dark that the Moon could hardly be seen with the naked eye, but on most occasions the very bright and very dark features, such as maria and ray craters, are visible with binoculars.

Unlike solar eclipses, lunar eclipses look the same from everywhere that the Moon is above the horizon.

Occultations by the Moon

As the Moon (and a planet too, for that matter) passes along the ecliptic, it regularly moves in front of stars and blocks them from view. Such a phenomenom is called an *occultation*. Although occultations can be predicted many years in advance, there is always an uncertainty of one second or more in the exact instant at which the star vanishes or reappears.

Stars disappear at the eastern edge,or limb, which is invisible before a full Moon, unless the Moon is a crescent and its dark side can be seen faintly lit by *Earthshine*—sunlight reflected onto it from Earth. Dark-limb occultations are much easier to observe than bright-limb events, because the star is easily lost in the

▼ **By timing** the disappearance or reappearance of a star at an occultation, the Moon's position in its orbit can be accurately determined, since the star acts as a reference point in the sky.

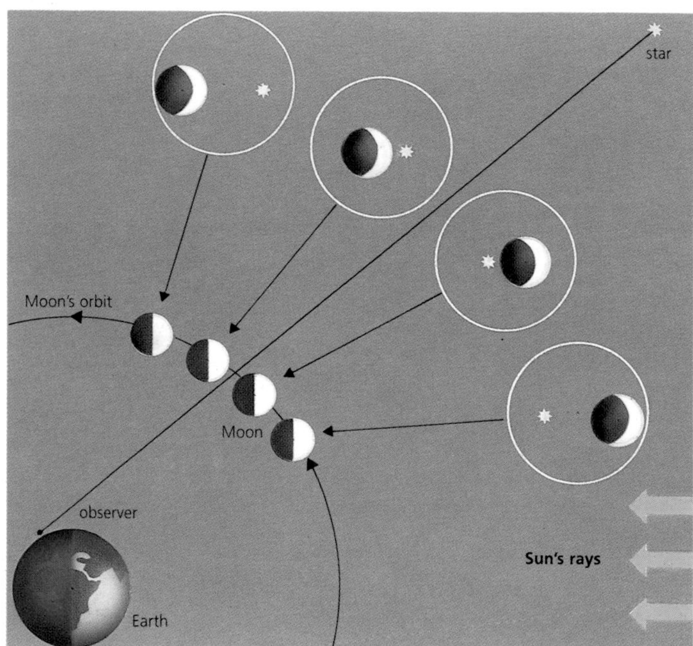

glare of the Moon. Planets are also occulted by the Moon, and it can be very exciting to watch as the Moon gradually covers the planet's surface. The Moon moves surprisingly fast, and even the large disk of Jupiter is completely covered within around 80 seconds.

▲ **A photograph** taken near last quarter, showing the terminator passing close to the Caucasus (upper) and Apennine mountain ranges. The 51-mile crater Archimedes, in the Mare Imbrium, is almost in darkness. Part of the Mare Serenitatis lies to the lower right.

Observing occultations

First of all, you need to know when occultations are expected: the information on page 172 tells you how to obtain occultation predictions.

Occultations of stars brighter than around 6th magnitude can be observed with a 60-millimeter aperture telescope, as long as the Moon is not too near a full Moon and there is no haze. To find the exact time at which a star disappeared, you will also need a stopwatch and the use of a telephone. Using the stopwatch, press the button at the moment the star disappears; then dial the telephone number of the automated clock. Stop the watch on a time signal—any one will work. Subtract the time shown on the stopwatch from the time given by the telephone clock to obtain the instant of occultation.

Pass your observations on to your local astronomical group. A lot of useful data about the motion of the Moon has been collected from occultation observations.

Amateur observation

Due to the *Apollo* landings between 1969 and 1972, we know a great deal more about the Moon's surface and interior than could have ever been found out from Earth. But the discoveries have been less sensational than those made about the planets, mostly because we have such an excellent view of our satellite.

Even the naked eye will reveal the dark lava plains, or *maria* ("seas"), and the bright uplands. Bright individual patches, such as the white deposit around Copernicus (lunar chart 3), can also be discerned.

It is interesting to compare the naked-eye view with a chart and to discover how much small detail can be seen. The bright crater Kepler (lunar chart 3) is more difficult to see than Copernicus, but the dark central sea, Mare Vaporum (lunar chart 2), is harder.

Remember that the charts show an inverted view of the Moon, to agree with the upside-down view of most astronomical telescopes.

▶ **The craters** of Fracastorius (lower) and Piccolomini are shown within the white outline relating to the waxing crescent Moon. The enlargement (opposite, lower right) allows comparisons to be made with a drawing of Piccolomini (opposite) by an amateur astronomer using a 200-millimeter telescope. The stages from outline to completion can be seen.

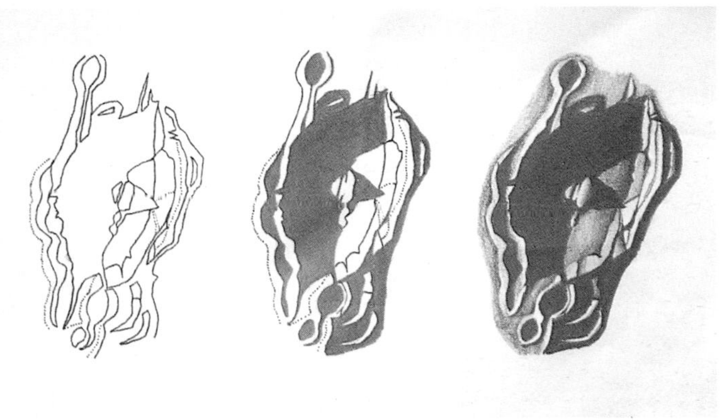

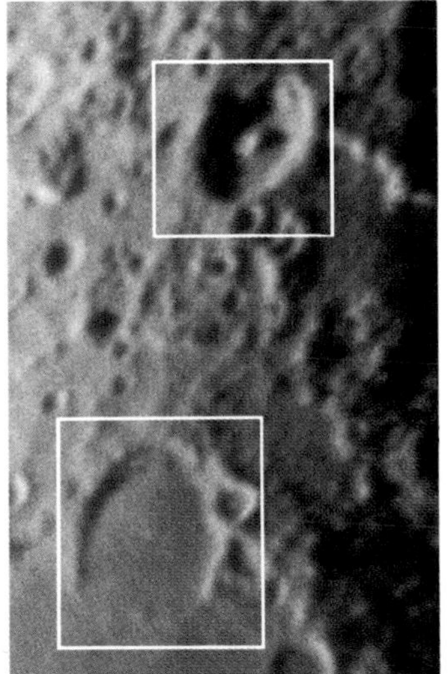

Binoculars or a low-power telescope show the main lunar features well, but for an adequate view of the craters and mountain chains in their true image, an aperture of 75 millimeters or more and a magnification of at least 100 is necessary. This gives a breathtaking view of the lunar surface.

The lunar charts

For convenience the Earth-turned surface shown on the charts that follow has been divided into four quadrants. Objects in the 1st and 2nd quadrants are the best when they are observed between new Moon and first quarter, when the Sun is rising over them, and again between full Moon and last quarter, when the Sun is setting. The 3rd and 4th quadrants can be seen under sunrise illumination between first quarter and full Moon, and under sunset conditions between last quarter and new Moon.

Lunar chart 1
Southeast quadrant

To aid with identification, the objects on these charts are shown as they would appear under sunset illumination, when they lie close to the terminator.

Rheita Valley: Best seen at four days old, this 99-mile (160-km) -long fault is never very easy to see because of its complex neighborhood.

Altai Mountains: Within this quadrant this is one of the more prominent mountain ranges. They look like the border of a wide, scooped-out valley and rise in places up to 2,480 miles (4,000m).

Theophilus: This crater, 62 miles (100km) across, has overlapped its neighbor Cyrillus, proving that it was formed at a later date.

Fracastorius: A good example of an old crater whose wall has been partially melted and broken down by fresh lava from the newly-formed Mare Nectaris.

Petavius: This makes an imposing sight with Vendelinus, Langrenus, and Furnerius along the terminator of the three-day-old Moon. Measuring 99 miles (160km) across, it has a wide valley running from the central mountain to the southwest wall.

Hipparchus: This and its neighbor **Albategnius** are both around 93 miles (150km) across and show all the signs of extreme age, having been dotted by meteoritic impacts long after they were first formed by gigantic collisions early in the solar system's history.

Stöfler: Prominent because of the intrusions on its east wall, this 50 mile (80km) crater can be recognized relatively easily, even in the chaotic terrain that characterizes the southern lunar highlands.

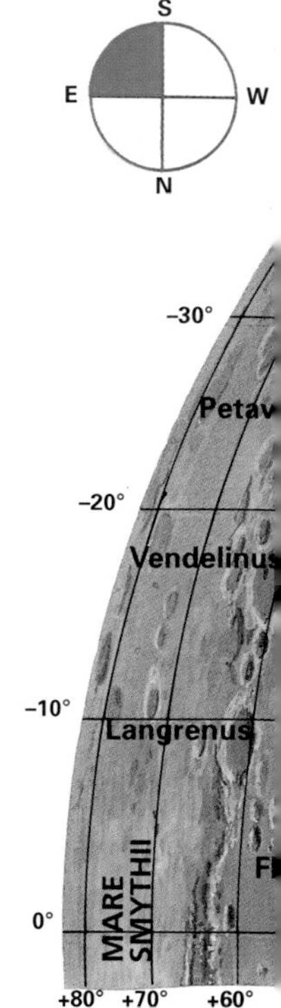

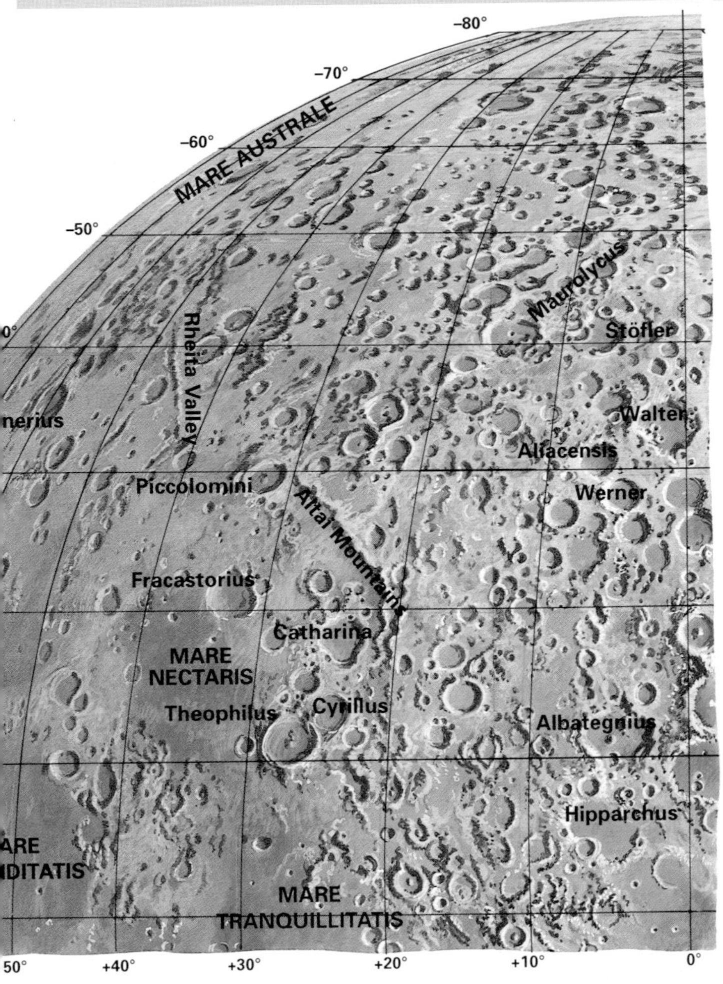
–80°
–70°
–60°
–50°
MARE AUSTRALE
Maurolycus
Stöfler
Rheita Valley
Walter
Aliacensis
Werner
Piccolomini
Altai Mountains
Fracastorius
Catharina
MARE
NECTARIS
Theophilus
Cyrillus
Albategnius
Hipparchus
MARE
TRANQUILLITATIS
50°
+40°
+30°
+20°
+10°
0°

Lunar chart 2
Northeast quadrant

Cleomedes: A magnificent 81 mile (130km) crater, spectacular around two days after a full Moon, when it and the Mare Crisium make an amazing sight.

Mare Crisium: One of the smaller seas at only 310 miles (500km) across, but very prominent. Its distance from the east limb changes a lot throughout the month, due to the Moon's *libration*—a slight swinging on its axis due to its changing orbital velocity getting out of alignment with its constant axial spin. Libration allows an observer to see a small part of the "invisible" hemisphere.

Mare Serenitatis: A partially mountain-bordered sea, it is best when it is seen at around five days old, when the surface is seen to be crossed by numerous ridges, as if it had wrinkled like skin over the still-warm interior.

Bessel: A small crater, only around 12 miles (20km) across, but easily spotted on the relatively crater-free surface of the Mare Serenitatis. A long, bright ray crosses both it and the Mare.

Endymion: Compare the dark floor of this 81 mile (130km) crater with its lighter neighbors, Atlas and Hercules.

Caucasus Mountains: These and the Apennines are among the highest, rising in some places to more than 19,680 feet (6,000m). They mark the boundary between the Mare Serenitatis and the Mare Imbrium.

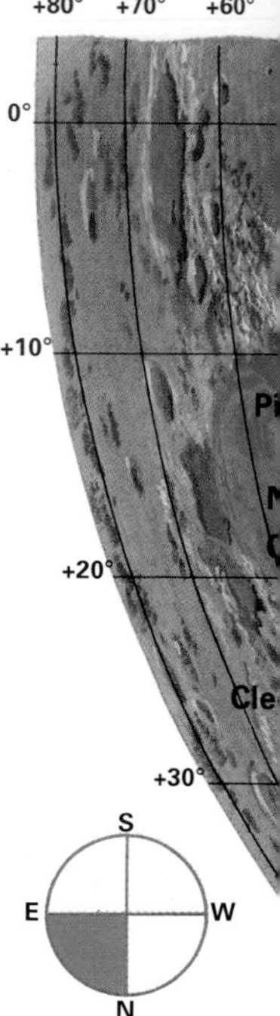

Hyginus Rille: A long valley that is visible at first quarter as a threadlike line, if a small telescope is used.

Alpine Valley: The Alps are not the highest mountain range on the Moon, but they contain the most extraordinary valley, 81 miles (130km) long and more than six miles (10km) wide. At first quarter it is visible with a 60-millimeter telescope as a sharp cut.

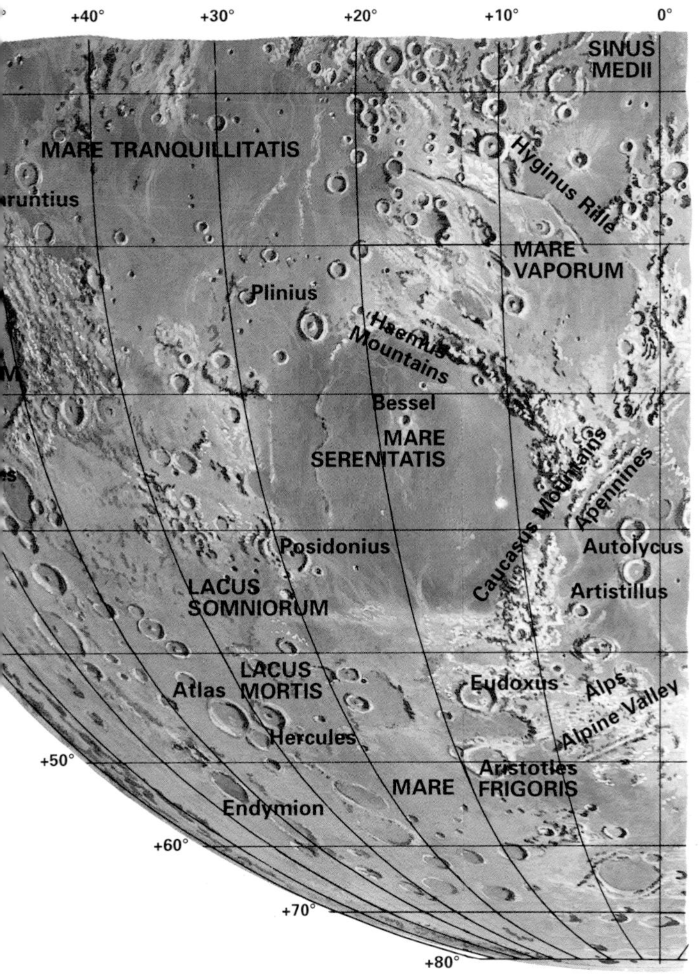
+40°
+30°
+20°
+10°
0°
SINUS MEDII
MARE TRANQUILLITATIS
Hyginus Rille
MARE VAPORUM
Plinius
Haemus Mountains
Bessel
MARE SERENITATIS
Caucasus Mountains
Apennines
Posidonius
Autolycus
Artistillus
LACUS SOMNIORUM
LACUS MORTIS
Atlas
Eudoxus
Alps
Alpine Valley
Hercules
+50°
Aristotles
MARE FRIGORIS
Endymion
+60°
+70°
+80°

Lunar chart 3
Northwest quadrant

Plato: A beautiful, dark-floored crater, 62 miles (100km) across. Evidently the interior was flooded by remelting.

Archimedes: This fine 56 mile (90km) crater, with its smaller companions Autolycus and Aristillus, makes an amazing sight just after first quarter. The floors of all three have been remelted, presumably by the same action that produced the Mare Imbrium.

Mare Imbrium: Perhaps the most beautiful of all the seas—as well as being one of the largest—measuring around 496 miles (800km) across.

Straight Range: A small, obvious group of mountains that stands up conspicuously on the Mare surface close to Plato.

Sinus Iridum: It was probably once a huge crater that was 155 miles (250km) across, but now one wall has been reduced by flooding, leaving a magnificent bay with peaks (the Jura Mountains) rising up to 19,680 feet (6,000m). When the Moon is around nine and a half days old, they can be seen with the naked eye, jutting out over the terminator.

Copernicus: One of the youngest large craters on the Moon. 56 miles (96km) across, it shows all the characteristic features: terraced walls, surrounding ridges, pits from the impact, a central peak, and the white rays that were caused by glassy, molten fragments that soared across hundreds of miles.

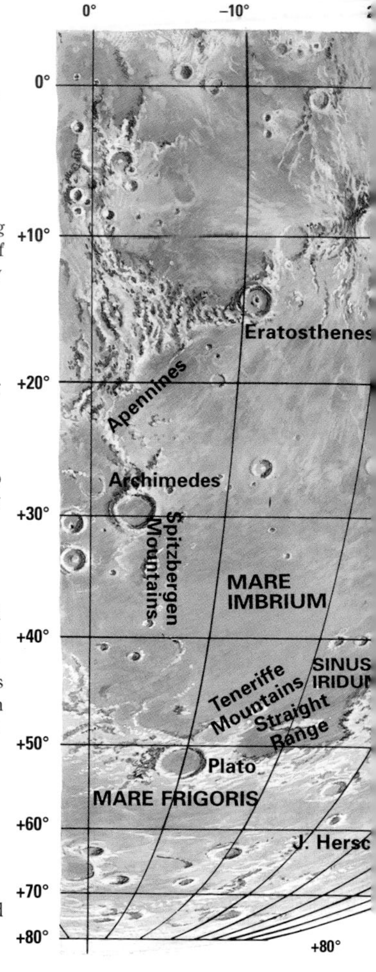

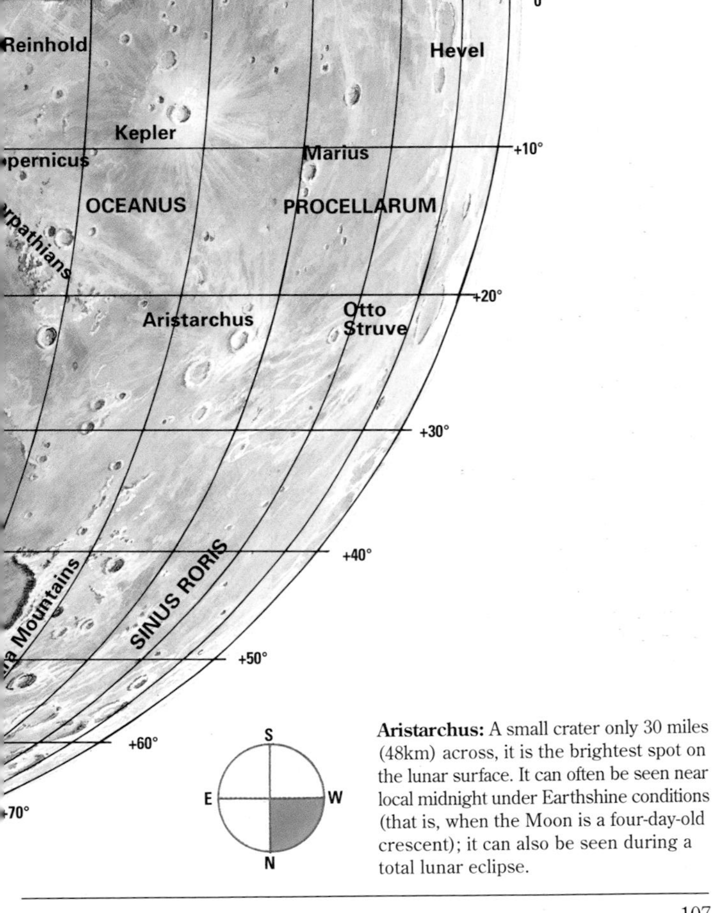

Aristarchus: A small crater only 30 miles (48km) across, it is the brightest spot on the lunar surface. It can often be seen near local midnight under Earthshine conditions (that is, when the Moon is a four-day-old crescent); it can also be seen during a total lunar eclipse.

Lunar chart 4
Southwest quadrant

Clavius: One of the largest lunar craters, 143 miles (230km) across, with a chain of more recently-formed craters inside it.

Ptolemaeus: This ruined 90 mile (145km) crater, together with Alphonsus and Arzachel, are imposing when they are seen just after the first quarter; the western walls are sunlit long before their bases are fully illuminated.

Oceanus Procellarum: The largest sea, but without mountainous borders, and much of it is featureless with a small aperture. There are many drowned rings where ancient craters have been submerged.

Grimaldi: A very dark crater close to the west limb and always obvious because of its tint. The slightly smaller neighbor Riccioli (99 miles, or 160km, across) is much harder to see, except just before a full Moon, when it lies on the terminator.

Gassendi: A beautiful crater with a flooded floor 56 miles (90km) across. Amateurs study Gassendi closely, as faint temporary red colorations have been reported here.

Mare Humorum: One of the better-defined small seas. A good sight on the eleven-day-old Moon, when tiny craterlets and ridges cover the surface.

Schickard: A dark-floored, 130 mile (210km) crater, ruined by later impacts. Note the curious object Wargentin to the southwest: a unique plateau,

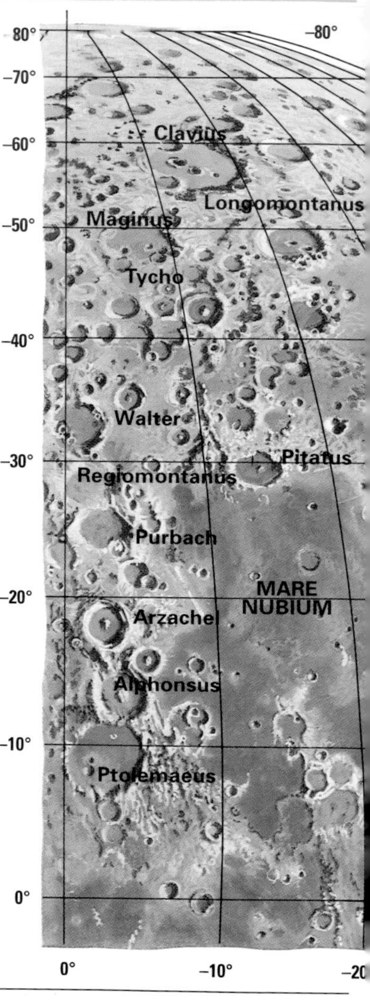

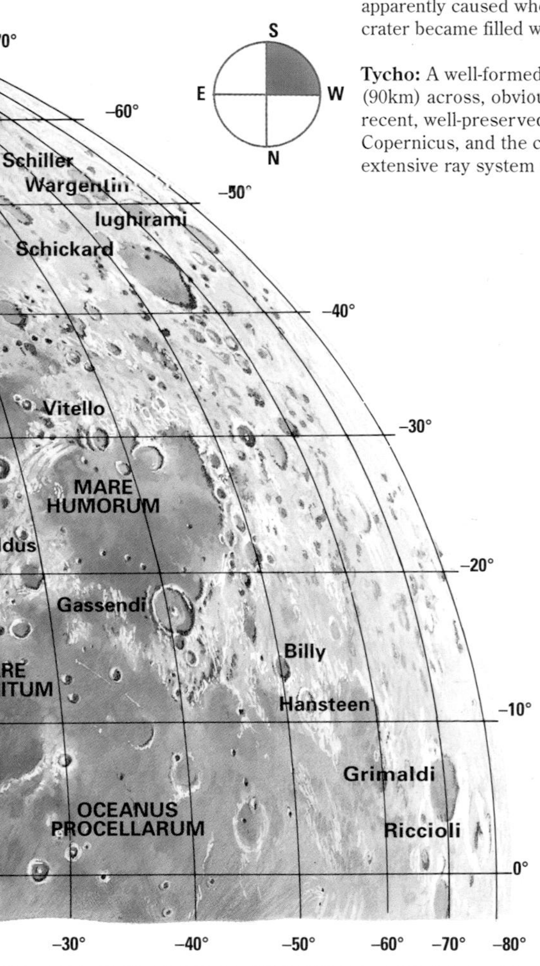

apparently caused when the original crater became filled with lava.

Tycho: A well-formed crater 56 miles (90km) across, obviously a relatively recent, well-preserved formation like Copernicus, and the center of the most extensive ray system on the Moon.

The planets

The planets have been mysterious objects ever since the ancient astronomers were puzzled about their movements across the celestial sphere. We now understand their wanderings; but as "worlds" there are still many questions unanswered about them.

The planets can be divided into two groups: the small or *terrestrial* planets, Mercury, Venus, Earth, Mars, and possibly Pluto, whose mass is in their solid globes; and the four *giant* planets, Jupiter, Saturn, Uranus, and Neptune, which predominantly consist of gas and have little or no rocky material.

The planets, satellites, comets, and scraps of debris that make up the Sun's family were all formed—together with our star—inside a huge cloud that probably consisted of 90 percent hydrogen, 9 percent helium, and traces of 90 other naturally-occurring elements.

Hydrogen and helium have fast-moving atoms that require a strong gravitational pull to restrain them. The Sun and the giant planets—Jupiter, Saturn, Uranus, and Neptune—were able to do so, and mostly consist of hydrogen. The smaller planets, like Earth, lost their hydrogen early and are dense, rocky bodies.

Planet fragments

Many other bodies also condensed from the original solar nebula. Some became satellites of the planets, while other smaller pieces are the billions of minor planets, or *asteroids*, mostly orbiting in the region between Mars and Jupiter. Innumerable billions of dust-sized fragments, *meteoroids*, circle the Sun invisibly, unless they burn up as *meteors* in Earth's atmosphere. A belt of around 60,000 icy space rocks orbits from Neptune's orbit to far beyond Pluto's orbit Finally there are the trillions of comets—icy and vaporous—that brighten to visibility only as they sweep close to the Sun during their lonely passage.

A question that intrigues every astronomer is whether there is or has been any form of life on the planets or moons in the solar system.

▶This view of the Sun and planets shows how small Earth is compared with the four "giant planets." But even the giants are tiny compared to the Sun.

The nine planets in the solar system are:

1 Mercury	2 Venus	3 Earth
4 Mars	5 Jupiter	6 Saturn
7 Uranus	8 Neptune	9 Pluto

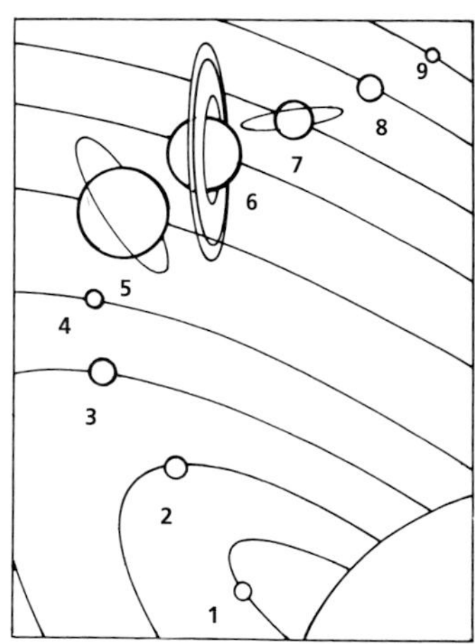

SOLAR SYSTEM FACTS

planet	distance from Sun (m. of km) min.	mean	max.	diameter (km)	length of day (hrs., mins.)	length of year (days, yr.)	no. of satellites
Mercury	46	58	70	4,850	176 d	88 d	0
Venus	107.5	108	109	12,104	114 d	225 d	0
Earth	147	149.5	152	12,756	24 h	365 d	1
Mars	206.5	228	249	6,790	24 h 37 m	687 d	2
Jupiter	741	778.5	815.5	142,600	9 h 50 m	11.9 y	63
Saturn	1,347	1,427	1,507	120,200	10 h 14 m	29.5 y	47
Uranus	2,735	2,870	3,004	51,000	17 h 18 m	84 y	27
Neptune	4,456	4,497	4,537	49,500	16 h 7 m	165 y	13
Pluto	4,425	5,900	7,357	2,280	6 d 9 h	248 y	1

▲ **Spacecraft** have photographed many planets and satellites. The results suggest that every solid surface in the solar system, including Earth's, was bombarded by small interplanetary bodies in Its early history. The photograph above is of Mercury's surface.

► **The surface** of Mars as seen from a *Viking* spacecraft.

◄ **A satellite** view of Mount Etna, Sicily, Italy. The radiation from different types of rock, soil, and vegetation, as well as human settlements, can be converted into false colors to aid mapping of surface resources.

Observing the planets

The planets are always fascinating to watch. Due to their orbital motion around the Sun, they are never in exactly the same position on the celestial sphere from night to night. However, different planets move in different ways.

Inferior and superior planets

Mercury and Venus, which are called the *inferior planets*, are a special case. Their orbits lie inside of Earth's, and so they are always in the neighborhood of the Sun. Pretending, for simplicity, that Earth is stationary, the lower left diagram shows how these planets move. First they pass from invisibility on the far side of the Sun, a position called *superior conjunction*, to eastern elongation, visible in the western sky after sunset. Then they go through inferior conjunction again, usually invisible, and out to western or morning elongation. During this time they pass through phases like the Moon, appearing full near superior conjunction and as a thin crescent near inferior conjunction.

The other planets behave as in the right-hand diagram. When they are closest to Earth they are opposite the Sun in the sky, like the full Moon—a position known as opposition; near conjunction they are invisible, behind the Sun. Only Mars sometimes shows a slight phase, near quadrature. These planets, from Mars to Pluto, are known as the *superior planets*.

The planets from Mercury to Saturn are visible with the naked eye; Uranus and Neptune can be seen with binoculars. Only Pluto is invisible without a decent astronomical telescope of around 250 millimeters aperture. Binoculars will reveal the crescent phase of Venus and up to four moons of Jupiter as well as one of

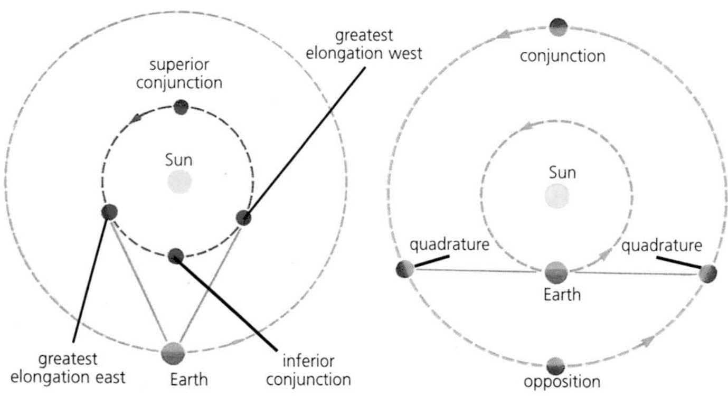

Saturn's moons. Binoculars are also a great help in finding "shy" Mercury during its fleeting appearances.

▼ **Binoculars** or a small telescope should reveal Jupiter's four large moons when they are near elongation from the planet.

▲ **A powerful astronomical** telescope will enable you to see a mass of fine, constantly-changing details on Jupiter's disk.

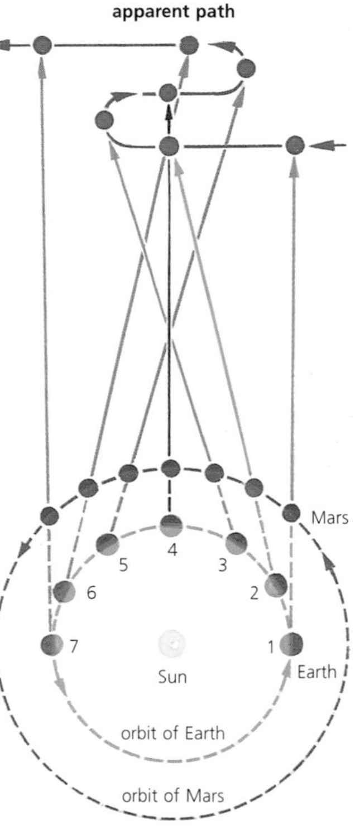

▲ **When Mars**, or any other superior planet, comes to opposition, Earth's greater orbital speed makes it appear to backtrack, or *retrograde*, for a few weeks, just as a car being passed seems to be traveling backward. This retrograde motion was one of the chief problems faced by the Earth-centered system of Ptolemy (page 22). The positions at 3 and 5, when the planet slows down and reverses its direction, are known as "stationary points."

Mercury

Mercury lies within 28° of the Sun and from temperate latitudes can only be seen in twilight, when it is near elongation. In the northern hemisphere the best time to hunt for it is from January to April as an evening object, and from July to October as a morning object. Reverse these times in the southern hemisphere.

Finding Mercury

Look about ten degrees above the Sun's location around three quarters of an hour before sunrise or after sunset. Times of forthcoming elongations are given in the sky diary (pages 160–162). But start looking for the planet about ten days before the time given. Mercury is white, but if you are looking for it in the evening, the sky often colors it pink.

Mercury shows such a tiny disk that a magnification of 250 only shows it as large as the naked-eye Moon. It was not until *Mariner* 10 visited it in 1974–1975 that much more was found out about it.

We now know that it is crater-ridden like the Moon. The next transits will be on November 8, 2006 and May 9, 2016.

▼ **Mercury** sometimes transits the Sun at inferior conjunction. This photograph was taken on November 10, 1973. The next transit will be on November 8, 2006.

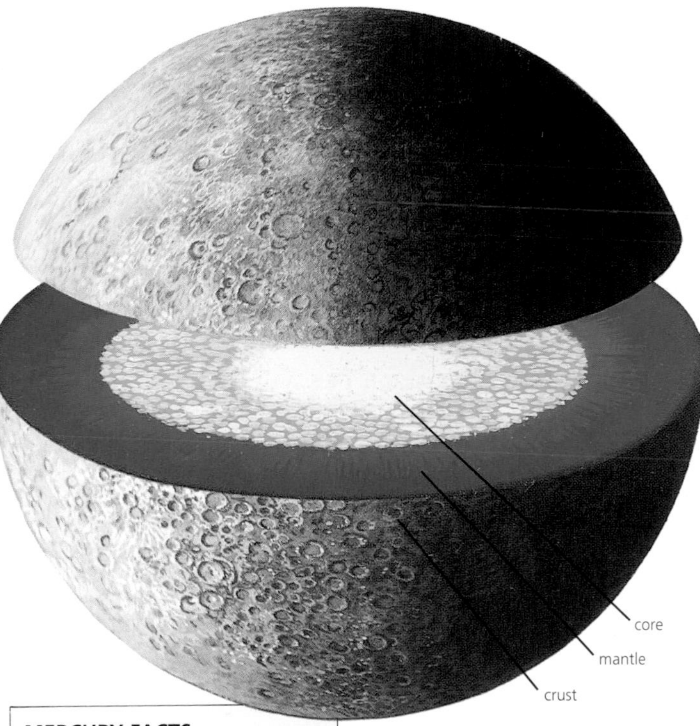

MERCURY FACTS

surface temperature: 662°F/-274°F
gravity: 0.8 × Earth
density: 5.4 × water
atmosphere: none
apparent diameter:
9" (inferior conjunction)
6" (superior conjunction)
interval between inferior conjunctions:
116 days
maximum magnitude: -1·4

▲ **Mercury** has an exceptionally large metal core, which makes it the densest planet in the solar system after Earth.

Venus

Like Mercury, Venus is an inferior planet, swinging into and out of the Sun's rays. It is much easier to see, however, and near elongation it can be seen with the naked eye in the daylight sky.

Phase and markings

Between elongation and inferior conjunction the crescent phase can be seen using firmly-mounted binoculars. It is at its brightest in the mid-crescent stage, and this is the best time to see it with the naked eye in daylight—perhaps at a morning elongation as the Sun rises.

It is no use observing Venus through a telescope in a dark sky, because its brilliance can dazzle you. The best time is in bright dawn or dusk, when it begins to be easily detectable with the naked eye. Cloud markings are very difficult to see, but occasionally observers have recorded hazy details that seem to conform to the streaks recorded by spacecraft. A blue photographic filter placed near the eyepiece should improve the contrast of any visible clouds.

Due to the way the atmosphere shades off close to the terminator, the phase of Venus is usually slightly less than predicted—on the date of the half-phase, for example, it may appear slightly concave rather than perfectly straight.

Rapid movement

Venus is usually lost from view for around four months, around the time of superior conjunction. But it sweeps through inferior conjunction so quickly that it reappears in the morning sky only a matter of days after it vanishes in the evening twilight. Venus is called the Morning or Evening Star, based on when it is visible.

▼ **The phases of Venus**. Venus goes through a phase cycle that is similar to the Moon's. When Venus is closest to Earth, only a part of its sunlit surface is turned Earthward (top row). More of its lit surface is visible when it is farther away, but Venus appears smaller because of its increased distance (bottom row).

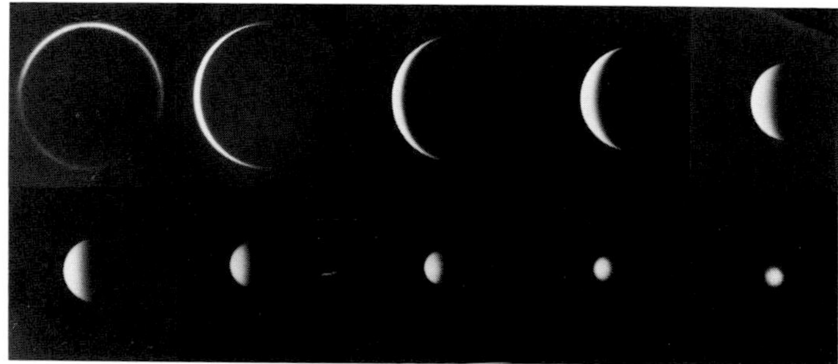

VENUS FACTS

surface temperature: 896°F
gravity: 0.9 × Earth
density: 5.2 × water
atmosphere: mainly carbon dioxide
atmospheric pressure: 91 × Earth's
apparent diameter:
62" (inferior conjunction)
10" (superior conjunction)
interval between inferior conjunctions:
584 days
maximum magnitude: -4·4

▲ **Venus'** internal structure is probably similar to that of Earth, but its surface has developed in a different way. There is evidence that its crust may have completely melted a few hundred million years ago, erasing all the older features.

Mars

Mars is the only planet in the solar system that gives us a reasonable view of its actual surface. But because it is so rarely in a good location for observation, it has puzzled rather than informed both amateur and professional astronomers.

Mars comes to opposition every 26 months or so, but its orbit is so erratic that some apparitions bring the planet much closer than others do. In 1971 it came within 35 million miles of Earth, but in 1980 its opposition distance was around 62 million miles.

Observation hints

All of this means that observing Mars can be frustrating. Really favorable oppositions occur at intervals of around 17 years: the last one was in 2003. Mars also approaches and recedes so rapidly that useful work can only be carried out for a few weeks. When it does appear, you can try to follow its rapid path with binoculars.

▼ **The face of Mars**. Images from the 1976 *Viking Orbiter* spacecraft, showing the system of canyons known as the Valles Marineris.

▼ **Mars** has a relatively small metallic core.

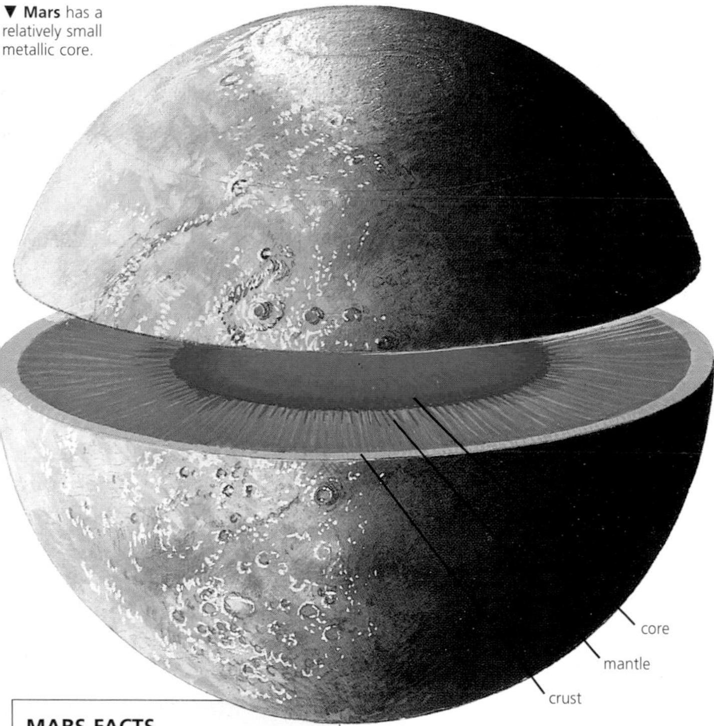

MARS FACTS

surface temperature: -4°F/-328°F
gravity: 0.38 × Earth
density: 3.95 × water
atmosphere: very thin, mainly carbon dioxide
apparent diameter: 14"–25" (opposition)
3" (conjunction)
interval between oppositions: 780 days
maximum magnitude: -2·5

With telescopes of 60 millimeter aperture you can look for dark markings and the polar caps. Try following a dark marking for around one hour. It will move with the planet's rotation from east to west (right to left in the telescope).

The deceptive planet

In 1886 the American observer Percival Lowell built an observatory in Arizona that was dedicated to the study of Mars. This was a time when astronomers knew little about the conditions on other planets, and Mars was widely thought of as an Earthlike world, where intelligent life could thrive. Lowell believed that he had discovered dozens of artificial waterways or canals on its surface and that the planet was inhabited by intelligent beings. Unfortunately, the thin, straight lines that were observed by Lowell and others do not exist. The tiny Martian disk had deceived them into imagining these features.

Mars' atmosphere

The atmosphere of Mars is very thin—less than one hundredth the density of our own—and mostly consists of carbon dioxide. But fierce winds can blow the dust into huge clouds that are visible from Earth by the dark features they obliterate; even the polar caps have sometimes disappeared. The strongest dust storms happen when Mars is near perihelion, at its closest to the Sun.

White clouds are also seen, usually near the planet's limb, where they can be almost as bright as a polar cap. Like the caps, they consist of ice. There could also be a good deal of water that is permanently frozen below the surface.

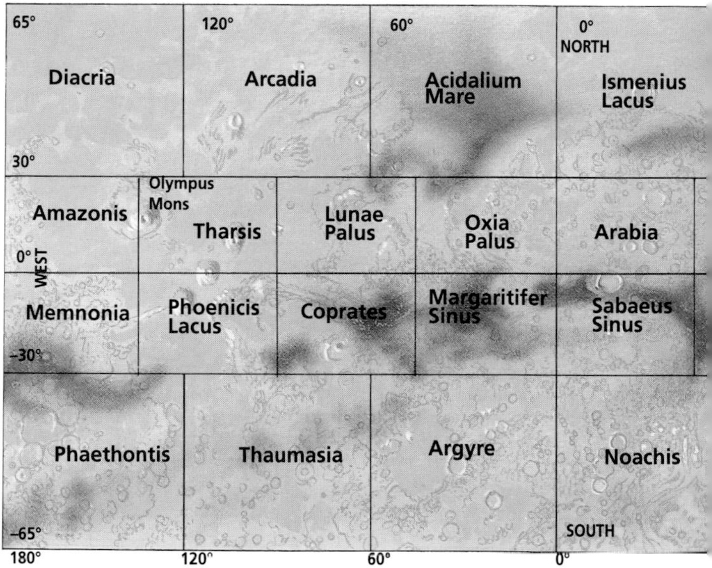

Life on Mars

We have not yet answered the question as to whether there is—or ever was—life on Mars. The present conditions on Mars do not seem suitable, but primitive organisms may have survived there in the past. Around 3.5 billion years ago it was a much warmer place, with liquid water on its surface.

The two Viking probes looked for signs of life in 1976, but no conclusive evidence was found at their landing sites. However, the surface of Mars is so varied that some other regions may be more hospitable. Within the past decade three rovers have explored new areas. In time other probes will be sent to Mars, one of which may provide the answer.

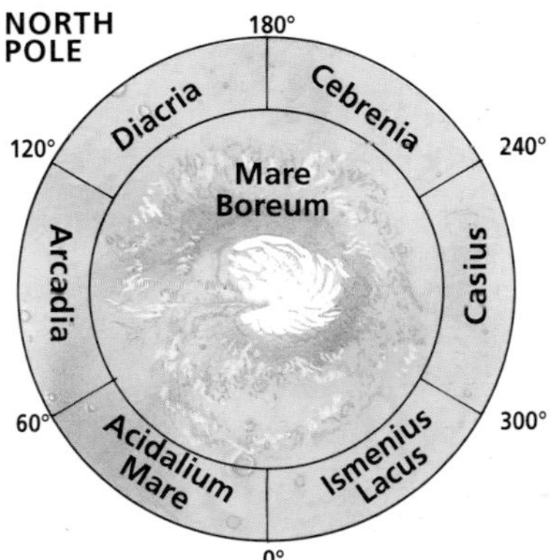

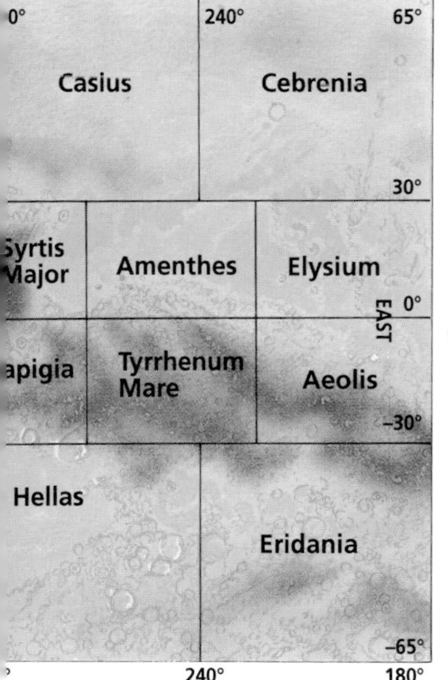

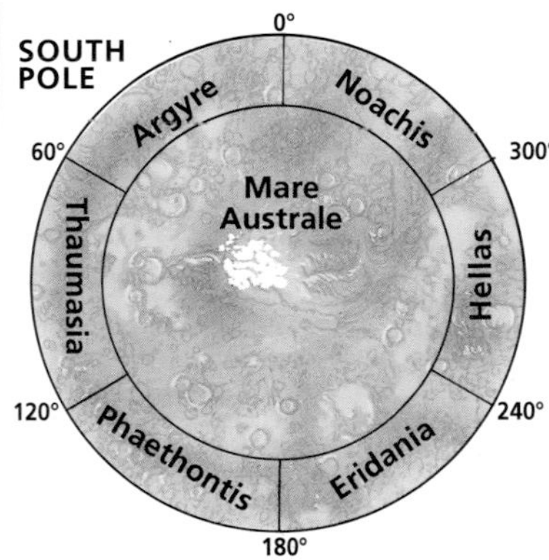

These maps show the surface of Mars, as photographed by space probes. The dark areas that are visible from Earth are shaded in. Two of the most obvious features are the dark Syrtis Major and the light Hellas. The huge volcano on the Tharsis-Amazonis ridge, Olympus Mons, is around 16 miles (25km) high with a crater at the top that is 40 miles (65km) across.

Jupiter

Jupiter is an ideal planet for an amateur astronomer to observe. Its disk is always large (even a magnification of around forty makes it look as big as the Moon), and there are four bright satellites. In outward order from the planet these are Io, Europa, Ganymede, and Callisto. They can all be seen using good binoculars.

With an aperture of 60 millimeters and a magnification of 100 or so, details are visible on the "surface" (really the upper cloud layer). The belts show wisps and irregularities, and the famous Great Red Spot can be seen when it is prominent, although it sometimes fades from view.

Jupiter spins so rapidly that its disk is noticeably flattened at the poles. A watch of between five and ten minutes will show that its markings are moving from east to west across the disk, due to its rotation. The longitude of a cloud feature can be figured out by timing the moment when it crosses the planet's central line, or meridian.

Observing the satellites

You can also observe the four largest satellites as they move around the planet. Try timing their orbital paths by seeing how long they take to return to a chosen position. Try to see their shadows as they move across Jupiter's disk.

▼ **Jupiter** may have a rocky or metallic core around the size of Earth, but it is principally made of hydrogen, compressed into a liquid by the enormous pressure of the outer layers.

▲ **Jupiter**, as viewed from a *Voyager* spacecraft, showing the Great Red Spot and one of the satellites. The immense amount of detail here cannot be duplicated by any Earth-based telescope, but these "brilliant glimpses" do not challenge the long-term monitoring of its cloud changes by a small team of dedicated amateurs.

JUPITER FACTS

temperature at cloud tops: -238°F
gravity: 2.7 × Earth
density: 1.3 × water
atmosphere: hydrogen, helium
apparent diameter:
47" (opposition)
32" (conjunction)
interval between oppositions:
399 days
maximum magnitude: -2·5

Saturn

Saturn used to be known as "the planet with the rings," but now we know that it shares this distinction with Jupiter, Uranus, and Neptune. However, the rings around these other planets are so faint that they have never been seen by the naked eye, whereas Saturn's rings are one of the glories of the night sky.

Earth-based telescopes can distinguish three main rings, but the two *Voyager* spacecraft have revealed hundreds of strands that are only a couple miles wide; some are concentric, while others are braided together.

The rings lie in the plane of Saturn's equator. Its axis is tilted so that during its long "year" we see the rings at different angles. In 2003 the southern face was tilted with its widest angle toward Earth, while in 2009 the edges will be seen.

Markings and moons

Saturn's globe is even flatter than Jupiter's. Its rotation period is slightly longer, but it has very little rigidity—its average density is less than that of water. The belts are much more faint than those of Jupiter, and noticeable spots are rare. Saturn's most characteristic feature is the occasional production of a large white cloud in its northern hemisphere. Prominent clouds were observed in 1960 and 1990—the latter was discovered by amateur observers in time for it to be photographed by the Hubble Space Telescope. The intervals between these outbreaks is approximately equal to Saturn's year, and they occur when the northern hemisphere is close to "midsummer." Saturn has 47 satellites—38 have been discovered since 1980. They range from planet-sized Titan, 3,193 miles (5,150km) across, to potato-shaped objects only a few miles across.

► **Two close-up views** from *Voyager* of Saturn and its rings, showing the numerous ringlets.

▼ **Spacecraft** have discovered additional rings around Saturn: only the bright A, B, and C rings are easily visible from Earth.

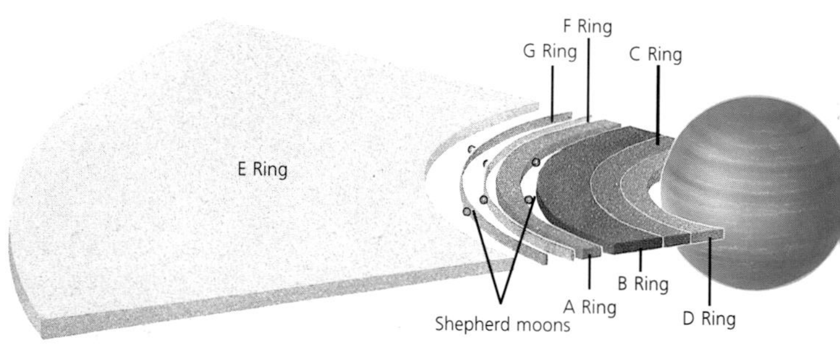

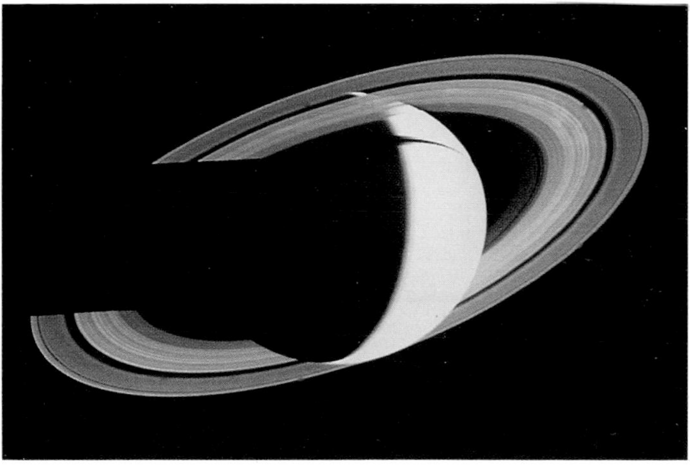

Observing Saturn

With the naked eye, Saturn looks like a yellowish star of around magnitude 2. Because it takes almost 30 years to pass around the zodiac once, it spends more than two years in each constellation. Saturn's 1996 opposition was in Pisces, and it only reached the neighboring constellation of Aries in 2000.

Saturn's rings can be seen with a magnification of around 50, unless they are almost edgeward facing, as happened in 1995. At this time they can briefly disappear from view, even in the largest telescopes, making the planet look like a small, flattened Jupiter. When they are wide open, Cassini's Division can be seen through a small astronomical telescope. Titan can be seen with good binoculars, and other moons can be identified with anything that is more powerful. Apart from a brighter equatorial zone and the dusky poles, it is usually difficult to see any markings on the disk itself.

SATURN FACTS

rings' inner edge: 4,112 miles from Saturn
rings' outer edge: 262,094 miles from Saturn
temperature at cloud tops: -292°F
gravity: 1.2 × Earth
density: 0.7 × water
atmosphere: hydrogen, helium
apparent diameter:
19.5" (opposition)
16" (conjunction)
interval between oppositions: 378 days
maximum magnitude: -0·3

▼ **Saturn is** probably built on a very similar pattern to Jupiter.

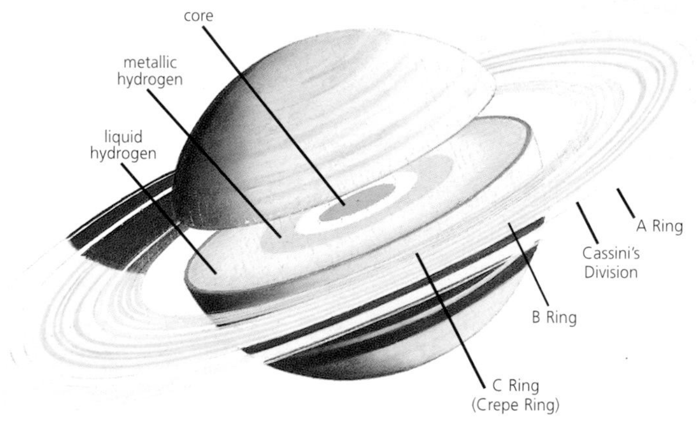

Uranus, Neptune, and Pluto

Our knowledge of Uranus and Neptune used to be scarce. However, we have been able to gain information from *Voyager* 2 about these two planets, such as their rotation periods and diameters. We still do not know much about Pluto.

Uranus is just visible to the naked eye, but it was not noticed until 1781. The discovery was made by William Herschel, who came across the planet in a survey of the sky with a 150 millimeter reflector. The belief that there were only five planets went back thousands of years, so at first Herschel found it hard to believe what he had found.

Neptune and Pluto were found after deliberate searches by astronomers who thought that the gravitational attraction of one or more unseen bodies was pulling Uranus from its theoretical position. Predictions by Adams and Leverrier led to the discovery of Neptune in 1846, and Pluto was found by Tombaugh in 1930.

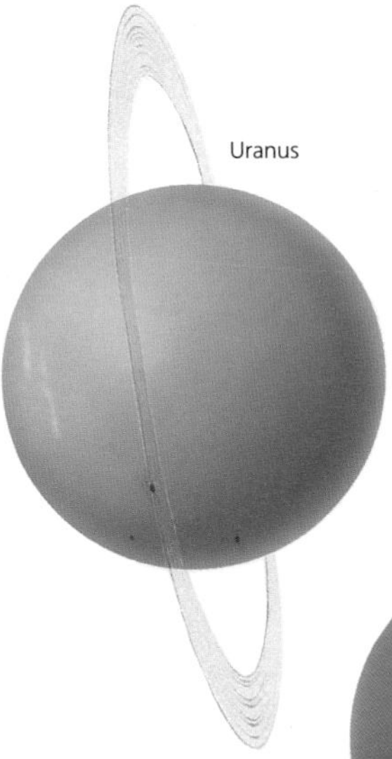

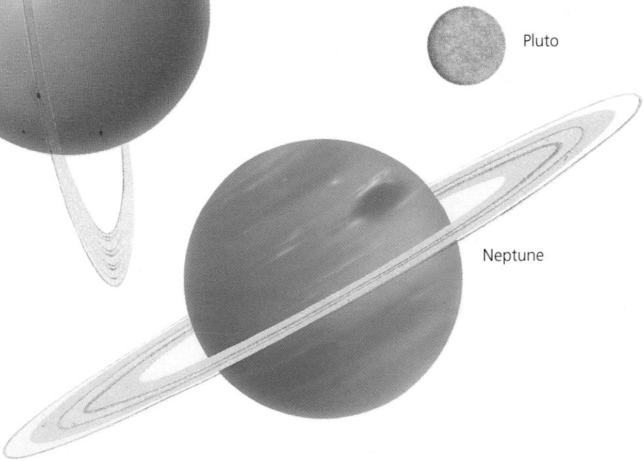

▼ **A drawing** of the distant planets (not to scale). From right to left: Neptune, Pluto, and Uranus.

Uranus

Pluto

Neptune

Rings and satellites

Both Uranus and Neptune seem to be built on the giant-planet pattern. They each have small, solid cores with thick layers of hydrogen, helium, and methane (a compound of hydrogen and carbon) forming an icy, slushy covering. Both planets have narrow ring systems. The axis of Uranus is tilted so far over that each one of its poles in turn almost faces the Sun for a while during its long year.

Uranus has 27 known moons, and Neptune has 13. One of Neptune's moons, Triton, is slightly larger than our moon, and *Voyager* 2 recorded jets of nitrogen gas spurting up from its surface. Winds rip through the outer methane atmosphere of Neptune at up to 1,362 mph (2,200km/h).

Pluto has a satellite named Charon, which is half its own diameter. Pluto's orbit is so eccentric that between 1979 and 1999 it was closer to the Sun than Neptune was. In 1992 the first of the icy rock bodies that orbit beyond Pluto—the Kuiper Belt Objects—was discovered.

Observation hints

Both Uranus and Neptune can be seen with binoculars if their position in the sky is known. But you will need to refer to astronomical yearbooks (see page 172) to know where in the sky to start hunting for them.

▲ **The face of Uranus** shows an unbroken haze in this photograph taken by *Voyager* 2 in January 1986.

◀ **Neptune** is revealed in detail by *Voyager 2* in August 1989. Bright, wispy clouds are shown overlying the Great Dark Spot at its southern margin and over its northwest boundary.

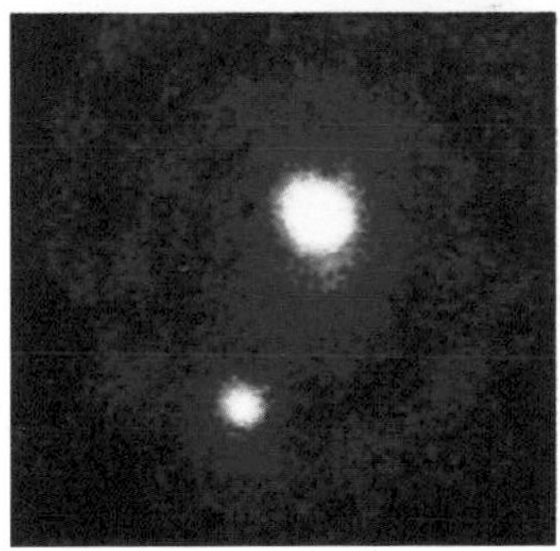

▶ **Pluto** is smaller than our moon and denser than any of its neighbors. It is often referred to as a double planet because of its very large moon, Charon. Pluto is the only planet that has not been visited by spacecraft.

Solar system debris

The planets of the solar system formed when tiny particles inside the solar nebula began adhering together. In some cases the process was halted before it had progressed very far, and small bodies a couple of miles across were all that resulted. Larger bodies probably collided and broke apart. The result of these misfortunes is the zone of asteroids, or minor planets, which lies between the orbits of Mars and Jupiter.

Asteroids

The largest asteroid, Ceres, is 620 miles (1,000km) across, but most of the 50,000 or so that have been discovered are much smaller. Vesta, 335 miles (540km) across, can sometimes reach 6th magnitude, and around a dozen can be seen using binoculars. A few asteroids orbit close to Earth: in December 1994 an object the size of a house, 1994XM, missed our planet by only 62,000 miles (100,000km).

▼ **Gaspra**, an object around 12 miles (20km) long, was the first asteroid to be photographed in detail when the *Galileo* spacecraft passed it in October 1991 on its way to Jupiter.

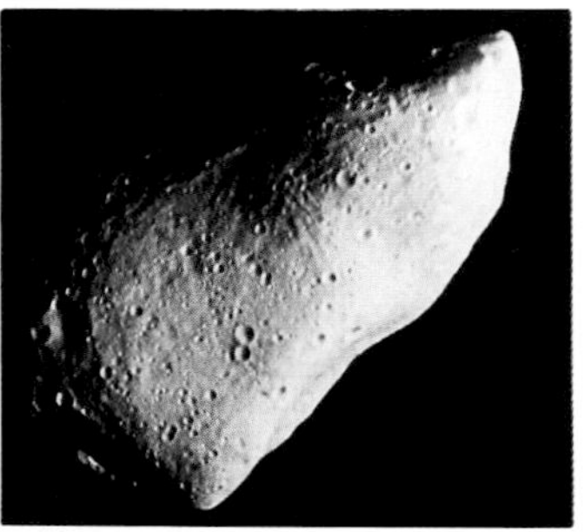

▲ **This brilliant fireball** was accidentally caught by an amateur photographing the stars.

Observing asteroids

An asteroid can only be distinguished from a star by its nightly motion, or by using a good star atlas. If its approximate position in the sky is known, an accurate drawing of the star field will show one "star" to have shifted. Asteroids will also show up as short streaks in long-exposure photographs taken anywhere near the ecliptic.

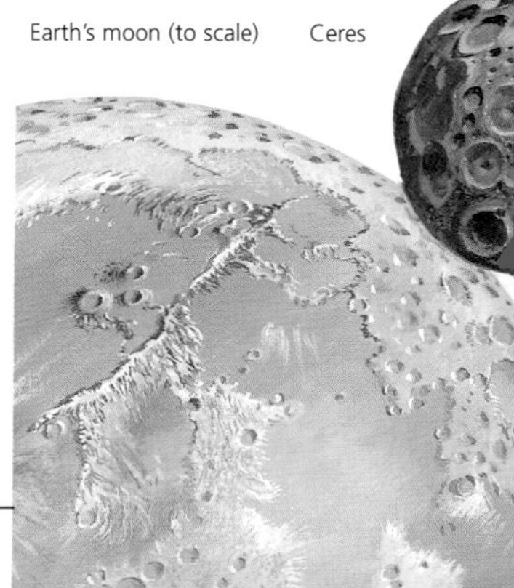

▼ **Most known asteroids** stay in the shaded zone, but Hidalgo, Apollo, and Icarus are three well-known exceptions. Two groups known as the Trojans survive in Jupiter's orbit.

THE ASTEROID BELT

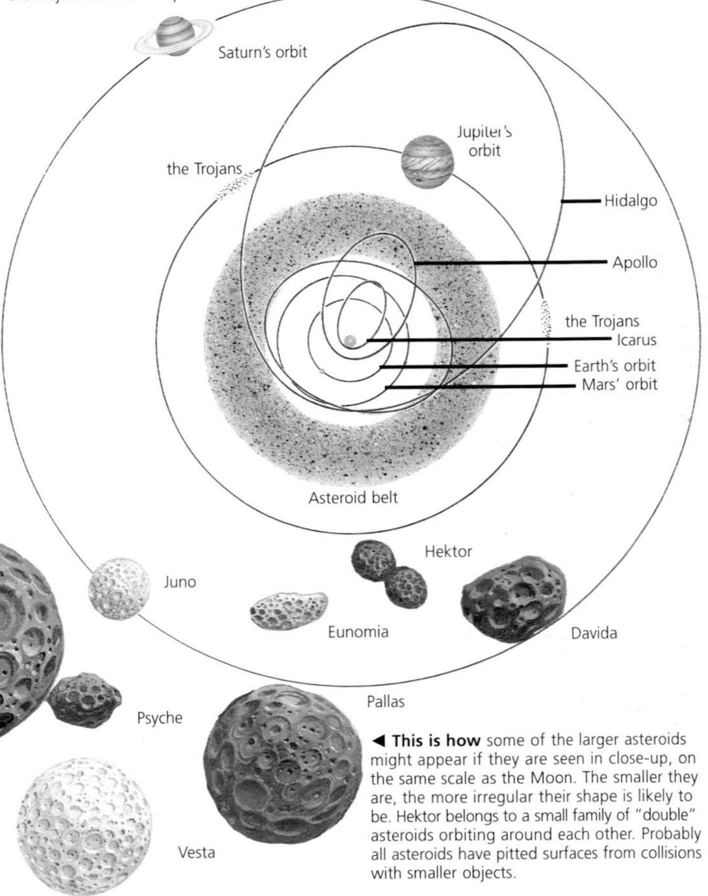

◀ **This is how** some of the larger asteroids might appear if they are seen in close-up, on the same scale as the Moon. The smaller they are, the more irregular their shape is likely to be. Hektor belongs to a small family of "double" asteroids orbiting around each other. Probably all asteroids have pitted surfaces from collisions with smaller objects.

Solar system debris

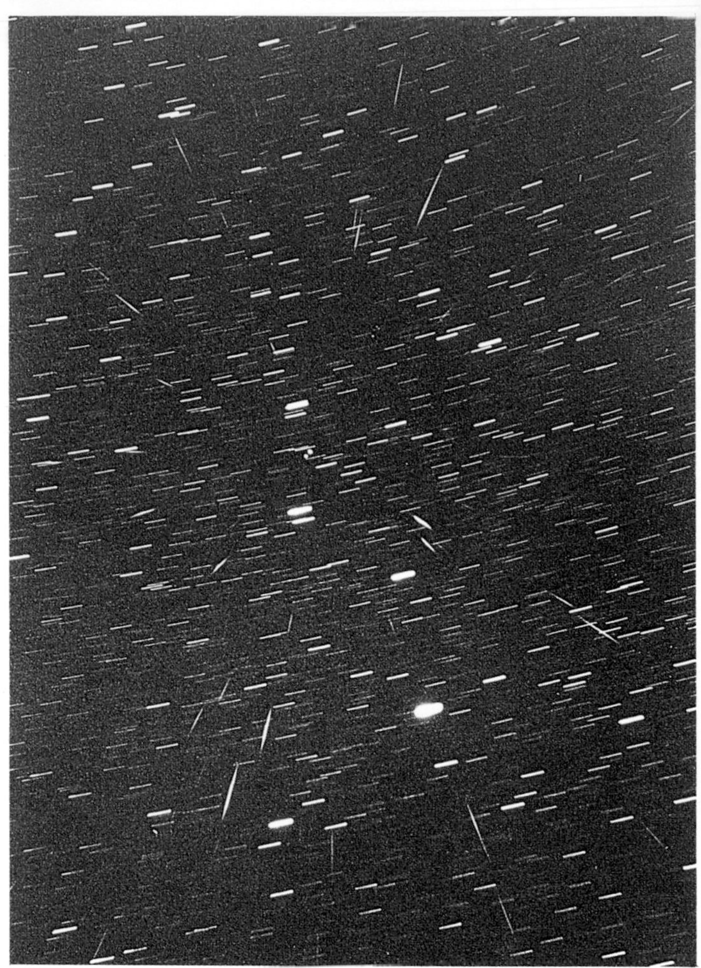

Meteors

Meteoroids—fragments of solid matter that are less than a couple of inches across—pervade the solar system. Some orbit the Sun independently, while others travel in swarms that have scattered themselves along a particular orbit.

Earth moves in its orbit at around 19 miles (30km) per second, and when it encounters a meteoroid, the relative velocity of the two bodies can be up to around 38 miles (60km) per second if it is a head-on collision. At these higher speeds the meteoroid is vaporized in the atmosphere, leaving the streak we see as a shooting star, or *meteor*.

Individual objects produce *sporadic* meteors. When Earth passes through a swarm, however, a so-called *meteor shower* occurs. This recurs every year when Earth returns to its intersection with the swarm. An estimated one million tons of interplanetary dust and meteoroid debris reaches Earth every day.

Earth sometimes collides with much larger bodies that weigh several pounds. These leave a bright streak that lights up the entire landscape and may even reach the ground as a *meteorite*.

◀ **This photograph** shows the tracks of numerous meteors that flashed across the sky during the brilliant Leonid display of November 1966. Such brilliant displays are very rare.

▼ **Meteor swarms** may be the dust of disrupted comets. A meteor shower is seen when Earth passes through this material that is scattered along its orbit.

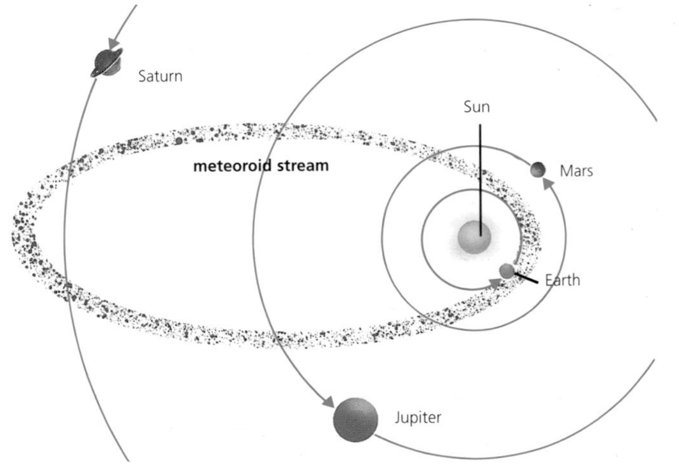

Solar system debris

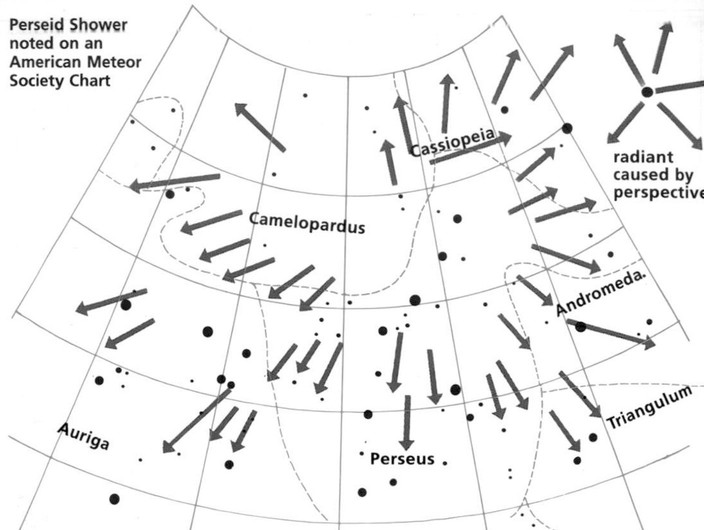

Observing meteors

Sporadic meteors can be seen on any clear night, but they are more frequent and brighter in the early morning. Meteor showers, however, only occur at certain times of the year (see the table on page 137). Bright moonlight can drown out less bright meteors, so observations are affected by the Moon's phases.

Observing a meteor shower is even more fun, and a group of up to six observers is best. Four people are each given one quarter of the lower sky, one looks overhead, and one writes details of the meteors that have been seen.

The most useful data to record are the time (to within half a minute), magnitude, speed (fast, medium, or slow), color, and whether a train (a faint trail) was left. It is also interesting to figure out how many meteors per hour were seen (the Hourly Rate or HR).

Experienced observers can try noting the meteor paths in relation to the stars. All meteor showers appear to come from one place in the sky—the *radiant*. The constellation in which the radiant lies gives the meteor shower its name. Often observers prepare charts in advance, like the one above, on which meteor paths can be marked.

► **This meteor crater** in Arizona may be 50,000 years old. It is 4,264 feet (1,300m) in diameter. On the Moon, because of its lower gravity, the same impact would have produced a much larger crater.

METEOR SHOWERS

Some meteor showers have very sharp maxima that only last a few hours, and these times vary from year to year because of leap-year adjustments. The sky diary (pp. 160–162) gives the best times at which to observe meteor showers such as the Quadrantids, Perseids, and Orionids. The two Aquarid showers are at their best when they are observed from the southern hemisphere.

shower	noticeable activity	maximum activity	maximum HR (approx.)
Quadrantids	Jan. 1 – 6	Jan. 3–4	50
April Lyrids	Apr. 19 – 24	Apr. 22	10
η Aquarids	May 1 – 8	May 4	10
δ Aquarids	July 15 – Aug. 15	July 27	25
Perseids	July 25 – Aug. 18	Aug. 12	50
Orionids	Oct. 16 – 26	Oct. 20	20
Taurids	Oct. 20 – Nov. 30	Nov. 8	08
Leonids	Nov. 15 – 19	Nov. 17	6?
Geminids	Dec. 7 – 15	Dec. 13–14	50

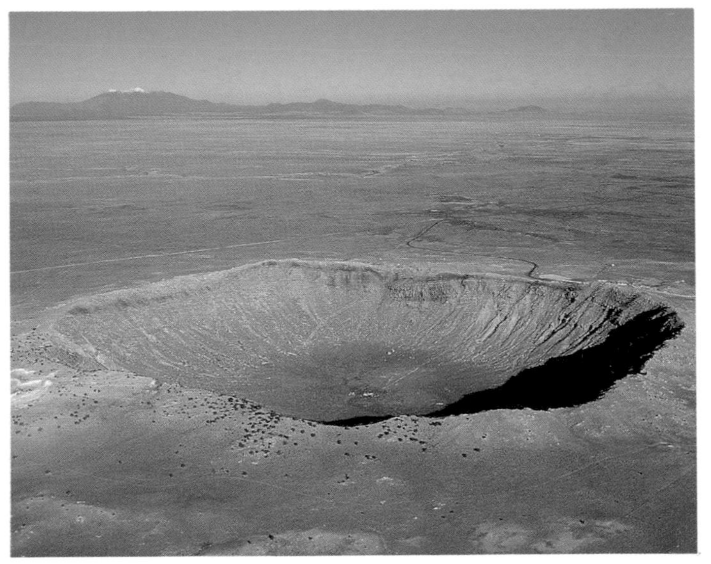

Comets

The popular idea of a comet is of a long-tailed object gleaming across the sky. But few of those that travel into the solar system achieve this distinction. Most are so faint that they can only be seen as a faint smudge, even with a powerful telescope, while countless more must pass through space undetected.

Comets are believed to originate in the Oort Cloud—a "halo" of trillions of bodies at an estimated distance of around 50,000 AU from the Sun. Rarely more than a couple of miles across, these were some of the first condensations within the nebula around the young Sun and consist principally of rock, ice, and snow, like a dirty snowball.

Occasionally one of these bodies starts to "fall" toward the Sun, a process that takes millions of years. As it heats up, the frozen material vaporizes, releasing the crumbly dust that it has been cementing together. The dust and vapor form a huge cloud, or coma, around the solid nucleus, and the Sun's continuous outflow of atomic particles may sweep this material into one or more tails that are millions of miles long. After hurtling around the Sun for several years—perhaps even closer than the planet Mercury—the comet recedes back into interstellar space.

▶ **Jupiter's powerful gravitational influence** on comets was spectacularly demonstrated in July 1994. Two years earlier its pull had forced Comet Shoemaker-Levy 9 into a collision course, breaking its nucleus into more than 20 fragments. This photograph shows the "fireball" in Jupiter's atmosphere soon after one of the fragments impacted.

▶ **One of the most spectacular comets** of the 1900s, Comet West was discovered by Richard West in 1976. For several days in March 1976 it was brighter than any planet, except for Venus, and could be seen with the naked eye. It was clear from its large dust trail that the comet's head was already breaking up.

The comet may return to the Oort Cloud, but it is also possible that the powerful gravity of the solar system giant planets—particularly Jupiter and Saturn—may deflect it into a much smaller orbit. This is the origin of the "short-period" comets such as Halley's Comet. Since they have made numerous passages around the Sun, a lot of their volatile material has already been blasted away, and they are relatively faint. The really bright comets, such as Comet West (1976) or Comet Ikeya-Keki (1965), have never previously been seen in recorded history and may have been making their first orbit of the Sun since the solar system began.

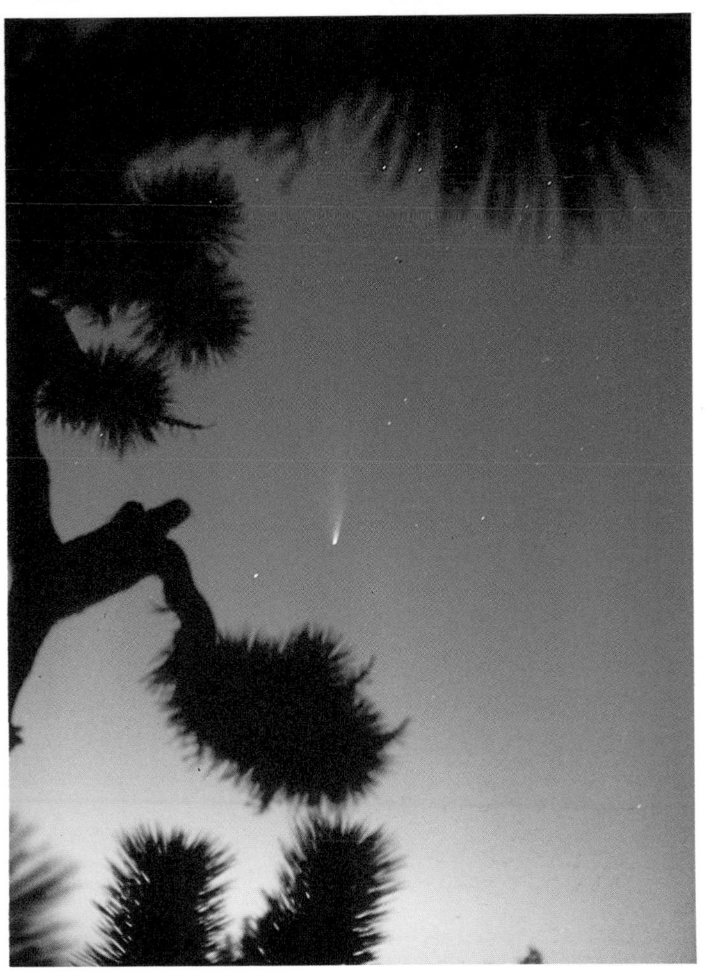

Solar system debris

Observing comets
Amateurs are still very successful in their search for new comets. This involves regularly sweeping the night sky with an aperture of between around 100 and 200 millimeters, with a low magnification, for example x 30.

Since comets are at their brightest when they are near the Sun, the western sky after dusk and the eastern sky before dawn are the most promising areas to search. A very dark, transparent sky allows for the best chance of making a discovery; but it may take some time. The most successful living comet discoverer is William Bradfield, an Australian amateur, who has so far found 18 comets.

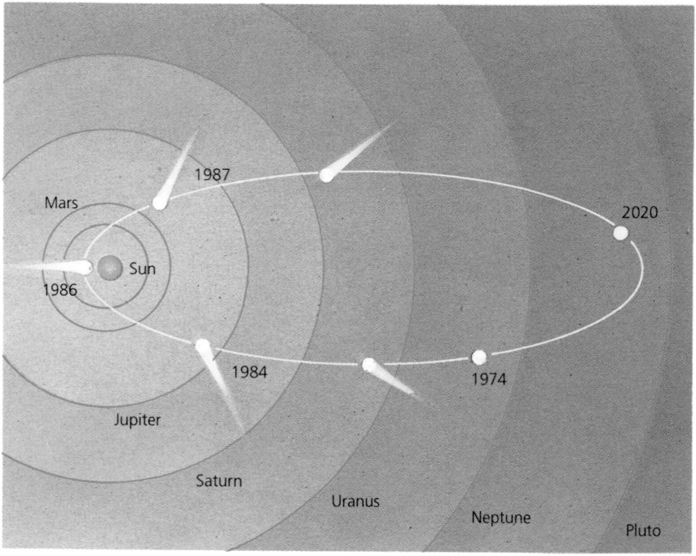

▲ **Halley's Comet** photographed in March 1986, three weeks after passing around the Sun. It appears an average of every 76 years.

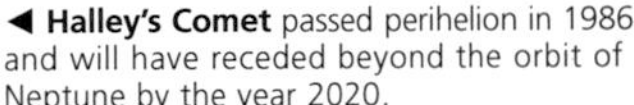

◀ **Halley's Comet** passed perihelion in 1986 and will have receded beyond the orbit of Neptune by the year 2020.

▲ **The dark, irregular nucleus** of Halley's Comet, recorded by the *Giotto* space probe in 1986, is around seven miles (12km) in length.

SOME IMPORTANT COMETS

name	orbit period (years)	last seen	comments
Encke	3.3	2003	Sometimes visible with binoculars; the shortest period known.
Biela	6.6	1852	Seen to break apart. A meteor shower occurred when Earth next passed its position.
Schwassmann-Wachmann	16.1	–	Always more distant than Jupiter and comes to opposition every year. Occasional outbursts.
Halley's	76	1986	Last perihelion passage in 1986.
Daylight Comet	750?	1882	Probably the brightest comet of modern times.
Donati	1,900?	1858	Famous for its curved tail, 40° long.
Daylight Comet	4 million?	1910	Probably the brightest comet of the 1900s.

Atmospheric astronomy

If Earth had no atmosphere (apart from the fact that life would then be impossible), the astronomer's task would be much simpler. The sky would always be transparent and free from clouds, and stars close to the horizon would shine just as brightly as those overhead.

But some features of the night sky would be absent. *Auroras* occur in the upper atmosphere and so do the rare *noctilucent* clouds. Other features, which we include under "atmospheric astronomy," although they really occur out in space, would be seen more clearly —particularly the *zodiacal light*, *zodiacal band*, and *gegenschein*, or *counterglow*.

▼ **Earth** has the most powerful magnetic field of all the terrestrial planets. Electrically-charged atomic particles from the Sun are trapped in different shells or are deflected into a "bow wave."

Auroras

Auroras are connected with solar activity. Close to ground level the atmosphere consists of nitrogen, oxygen, and other elements that exist as stable molecules. But at a height of around 56 miles (90km) the air is so thin that the molecules are split into atoms, which are broken down by the Sun's energy.

When the Sun's surface is particularly active, it radiates atomic particles that become trapped in Earth's magnetic field, rebounding from pole to pole and striking flashes of light from these high-altitude atoms. The result is an auroral display. Auroras mostly occur in the upper

► **A bright aurora** is a memorable sight. Displays are the most common around the time of sunspot maximum, when the Sun sometimes emits fierce bursts of radiation that makes atoms in the upper atmosphere glow.

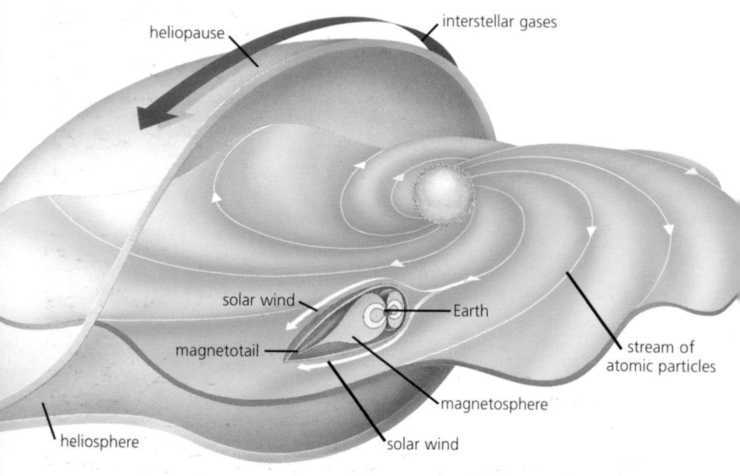

atmosphere close to Earth's poles, where the solar particles find an easier entry down through the magnetic field. Auroras can last for hours and be bright enough to be noticed by non-astronomers.

Observation notes

A faint aurora usually takes the form of a diffuse glow above the northern horizon (the southern horizon, in the southern hemisphere). It may develop rays extending up toward the zenith, and green and red tints may appear.

If you suspect an auroral display, make regular (for example five-minute) records of its height and extent along the horizon. The best latitude for auroral observations is around 60° north or south, but strong displays can sometimes be seen close to the equator.

Zodiacal light

Zodiacal light is caused when sunlight is reflected by interplanetary dust. It takes the form of a cone extending along the ecliptic. Since it is so faint, it can only be seen during a critical time between the beginning or end of twilight and its own rising or setting.

In higher latitudes it makes a low angle with the horizon and is difficult to see. In latitudes of around 35° and less it is bright enough to drown out the fainter stars and is known as the "false dawn."

Look for it in the west after dusk in the spring and in the east just before dawn in the fall (southern observers should reverse these times). A dark countryside sky is essential, and your eyes must be thoroughly dark-adapted if the elusive cone is to be seen.

Gegenschein

The gegenschein, or counterglow, is also caused by interplanetary dust, but it lies across from the Sun in the sky and appears as a very dim patch that is several degrees across. It is fainter than the zodiacal light or the Milky Way. The best time to observe it is around midnight. In the northern hemisphere look for it at the beginning of November, when it lies in Aries (star maps 2 and 3). The best chance for southern observers is in early February, when it lies in Capricorn (star map 7). There is no hope of seeing the zodiacal light or the gegenschein except for deep in the countryside, away from any source of illumination.

▼ **A diagram** to show how the zodiacal light appears in relation to the Sun.

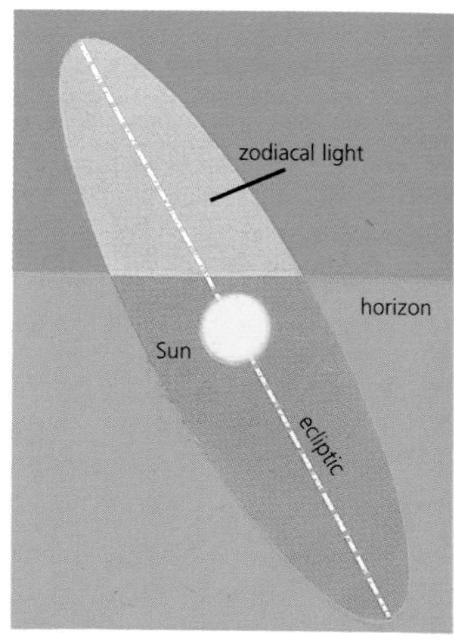

The Milky Way and beyond

▲ **A photographic "panorama"** of the Milky Way, as it might be seen by an astronaut out in space. The nucleus of the galaxy is toward the center, and the two small objects below it are our satellite galaxies, the Magellanic Clouds.

All the stars that are visible in the night sky belong to the Milky Way galaxy. Although it is such an obvious feature of a dark night sky, the Milky Way puzzled astronomers until far into the 1900s. It was known to consist of distant stars—but how distant, and what lay beyond? Was the universe just an endless succession of stars? The problem could not be solved by direct observation, because our position inside it meant that its form could not be seen. The position was similar to being in a crowd, unable to look over surrounding heads to see how far it extends.

The clue came when astronomers began to study certain hazy objects in the sky that had previously been taken as clouds of gas and dust, or nebulae. They realized that some of these consisted of stars that were so faint and closely packed together that they must be very distant star systems or galaxies. From this came the conclusion that the Milky Way was just one galaxy among many, and other galaxies could be used as prototypes to help classify it.

The galaxy is a pinwheel-shaped spiral, like the Andromeda galaxy two million light-years away. It is one of a group of more than 30 that form a big cluster, the Local Group. Most of the galaxies in the Local Group are elliptical-shaped dwarf galaxies, much smaller than the Milky Way. Our cluster measures around five million light-years across—not large compared with some groups, such as the Coma Cluster, which contains thousands of galaxies. Astronomers can see the brighter individual stars in these neighboring galaxies, and they are similar to those in the Milky Way.

The Milky Way and beyond

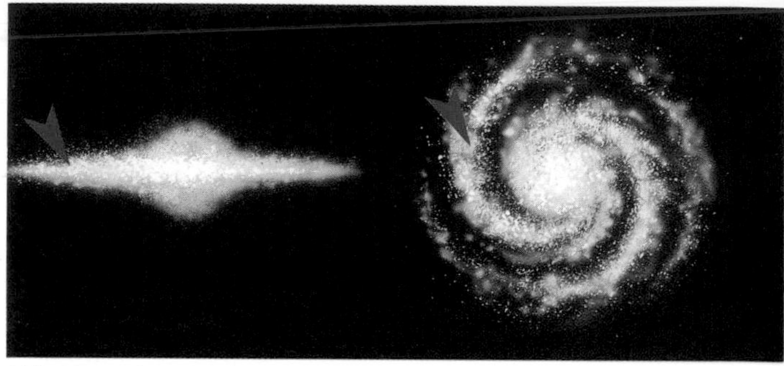

▲ **These two views** show how the galaxy would appear if it was viewed from out in space. From edge-on the galaxy looks like a flat disk with a swollen middle—the nucleus. From above, the galaxy looks like a whirlpool of stars. The position of the Sun, and therefore our solar system, is indicated in both views by red arrows. The galaxy contains at least 500 billion stars, but at least half of its material is in the form of nonluminous interstellar dust.

Galaxies in space

Galaxies are scattered throughout space as far as telescopes can reach, but it is not easy to measure their distances. For many years astronomers doubted whether any galaxies outside the Milky Way could be detected at all. For example, they thought that M31 in Andromeda was a local star cluster.

But in the 1920s it was realized that M31 must be remote, since Cepheid variables were discovered in it, looking much fainter than the farthest Cepheids found in our galaxy. Later on novas were also found, and their assumed absolute magnitudes helped place M31 at a distance of 2,200,000 light-years away.

Unfortunately, individual stars, such as Cepheids and novas, cannot be seen in very remote galaxies, and other methods must be used to measure their distance. One way is through the redshift relationship (see page 152). Another is to make assumptions about the absolute magnitude of the whole galaxy. (The absolute magnitude of M31, for example, is around -21, equivalent in brightness to 25 billion stars as luminous as the Sun.)

The difficulty with this method is that galaxies vary greatly in size and brightness. Some of the dwarf galaxies in the Local Group have absolute magnitudes as low as -9, which is not much brighter than a single highly-luminous supergiant star. Others are much more luminous than the Milky Way.

It seems that, although galaxies may differ greatly from one to another, the types of stars that they contain can all be found on the Milky Way-based Hertzsprung-Russell diagram. Star formation is a standard process throughout the universe.

▲ **The Whirlpool galaxy** (above left), M51, was one of the first galaxies to be identified. The Andromeda galaxy (above right), M31, is a bright nearby counterpart of the Milky Way.

▼ **M82 in Ursa Major,** an irregular galaxy around 8.5 million light-years away. The Seyfert galaxy (left) has an unusually bright nucleus.

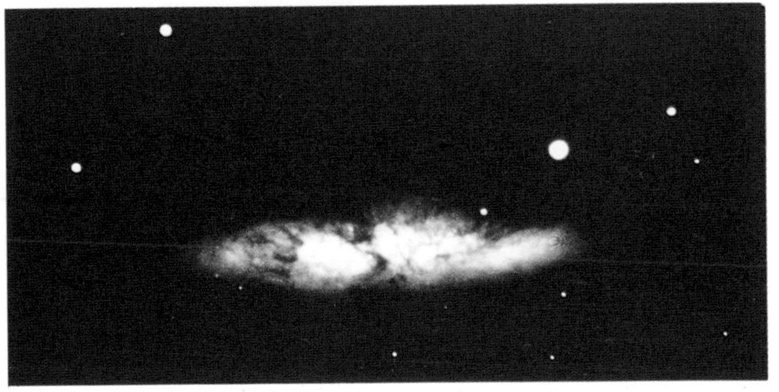

Classes of galaxies

Tens of thousands of galaxies have been photographed in detail, and most of them fall into the following classes: spiral (normal and barred), elliptical (like a spiral's nucleus, without arms), and irregular.

The star populations in these classes differ greatly. Irregular galaxies, such as the Magellanic Clouds, contain many young stars and nebulae (from which more new stars can form). Spirals have a mixture of young and old stars. In the arms there are young stars, Sunlike stars, dying white dwarfs, and nebulae. In the nucleus there are mostly old red giants.

Elliptical galaxies are the most common type and include some of the largest known objects, whose gravitational pull "sucks in" smaller galaxies. The stars are mostly red giants. There are also some very small examples, containing dim red stars: the faintest galaxies in the Local Group are of the elliptical class, as are the two bright satellite galaxies of M31 in Andromeda. The lack of dust and gas means that no new stars can be forming in these particular star systems.

▶ **The Magellanic Clouds** are visible to observers in the southern hemisphere.

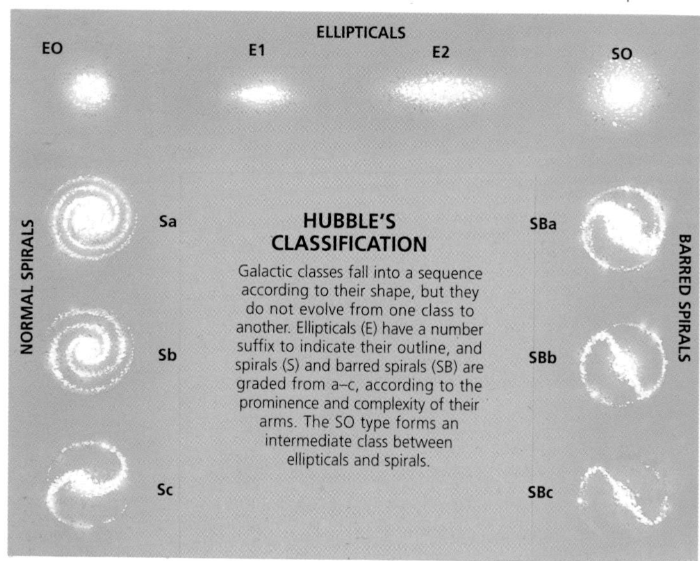

ELLIPTICALS
EO
E1
E2
SO
NORMAL SPIRALS
Sa
Sb
Sc
BARRED SPIRALS
SBa
SBb
SBc
HUBBLE'S CLASSIFICATION
Galactic classes fall into a sequence according to their shape, but they do not evolve from one class to another. Ellipticals (E) have a number suffix to indicate their outline, and spirals (S) and barred spirals (SB) are graded from a–c, according to the prominence and complexity of their arms. The SO type forms an intermediate class between ellipticals and spirals.

The Milky Way and beyond

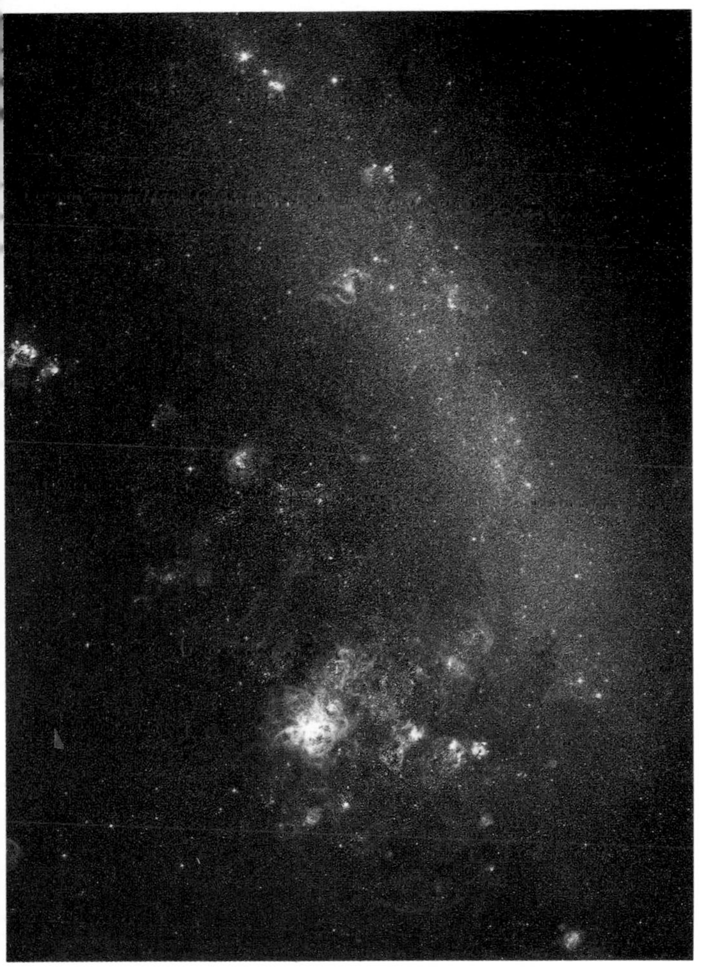

The Milky Way and beyond

Observing galaxies
Part of the fun of observing galaxies is the chase itself, since most are difficult to find and will even be a challenge for the most careful observer. A dark, moonless night is essential for this work.

The observation notes (pages 76–90) give a good sample of the brighter galaxies, but only one in the whole sky, M31 in Andromeda, can be seen with the naked eye. If it is in a good location, spend some time examining it with binoculars or a small telescope. It may seem like just a faint haze, but ask yourself the following questions, and others like them, and try to answer them accurately.

What shape is it? What direction is the long axis? What is the size in degrees or minutes of arc? How does the brightness change from the center to the edge? Is the brightest part in the center? Are there any dark or bright lanes or condensations? Are any stars close to it or projected onto it? Is any color detectable? If seen, what does the satellite galaxy M32 look like?

When you look at *anything* in the sky, ask appropriate questions like these. Your eyes will respond, and your observing will improve.

The origin of the universe

Most astronomers accept the idea that the universe is expanding from the *Big Bang*. Galaxies are flying apart, and if their tracks are run backward, they must have once been very close together.

It might sound simple to figure out when the expansion began, but astronomers disagree about how fast the galaxies are flying apart and how far away they are. However, an age of at least 15 billion years was accepted by most astronomers until quite recently, as the oldest stars seemed to be of this age.

The increasingly accurate observations of today's Earth- and space-based telescopes do, however, suggest that the universe is expanding quicker than it was previously supposed. It may only be twelve billion years old. If this is true, either some other factors have not been taken into account, or the oldest stars in our galaxy are younger than was previously supposed.

Physicists have tried to analyze what must have happened to the material that created what we now see as the universe. If all the matter that is present now was present then, the "primeval atom" must have been a mass of atomic particles at a temperature of *trillions* of degrees. Once it started expanding, however, the temperature would have dramatically dropped. Eventually the chaos of particles must have started arranging itself into the elements that we see today—hydrogen atoms being the simplest and by far the most common.

Evidence for the Big Bang theory comes from the discovery of faint radio waves that remain from the radiation that pervades space. The only satisfactory explanation is that they represent the last traces of the primeval atom explosion, the flash of immense heat that has almost faded away.

How the planets formed

The planets may have formed out of the "doughnut" somewhat like this. Remember that on this scale of the Sun's diameter, the doughnut would be the size of a small backyard.

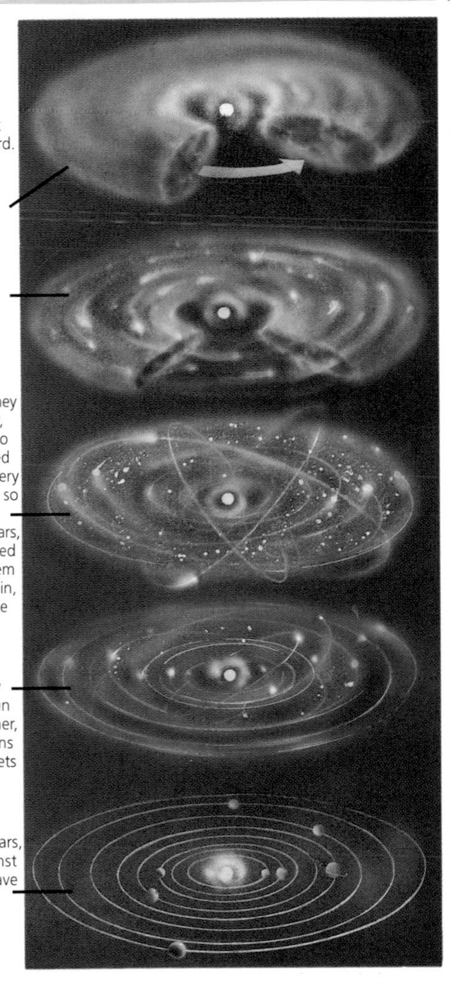

1 To begin with, the doughnut was a spinning ring of gas and dust.

2 The solid particles began striking each other and sticking together, forming larger bodies. At first these were mostly carbon and ice.

3 These particles rapidly grew to planetary size. As they grew larger they began to "pull" against each other, which meant that if they passed too close to each other, they were pulled into a different orbit. Some of the very small carbon-ice bodies were pulled so violently by the larger ones that they were thrown right out toward the stars, while others found themselves pulled into very long orbits that carried them far beyond the planets and back again, very close to the Sun. These are the comets (see pages 138–141).

4 Eventually there were only a few large bodies moving around the Sun in orbits that did not meet each other, and so there were no more collisions or near misses—the nine major planets were formed.

5 With the passage of billions of years, the planets continued to pull against each other, until now their orbits have become almost level.

Redshift

Light travels as tiny pulses moving through space at 186,000 miles (300,000km) per second. The color of the light depends on the distance between the pulses—the wavelength. If a light source, such as a star or a galaxy, is moving rapidly away from an observer, the wavelength is "stretched." A longer wavelength shifts the lines in the object's spectrum toward the red end, since red light has a longer wavelength than blue. All the clusters of galaxies in the night sky, except those in the Local Group, show redshift and by this indicate the expansion of the universe.

Those galaxies whose distances can be measured relatively accurately follow a law that says that the amount of redshift of the spectral lines is proportional to their distance. In other words, "the farther away, the faster it is." If this law is correct, the redshifts of very distant galaxies give a clue to their distance. The most remote objects that have so far been observed are probably 10–15 billion light-years away.

The "Hubble constant" is somewhere in the region of 31–62 miles (50–100km) per second.

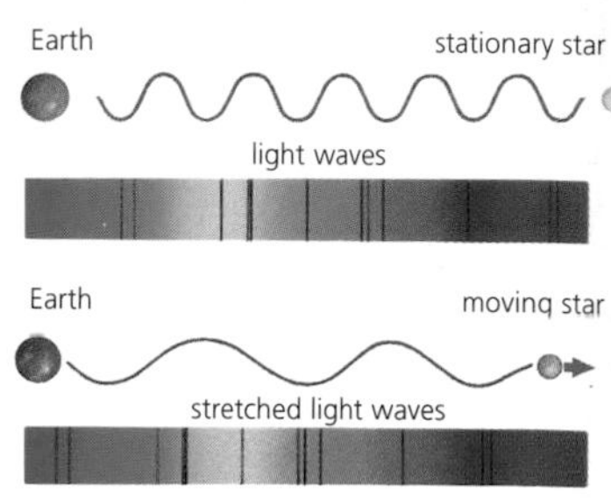

▲ **A shining body** emits electromagnetic radiation, which is energy pulses, or waves. If it is moving at a high speed, its motion increases or decreases the wavelength, as recorded by an observer.

galaxy moving away from Earth

◀ **Many people** think that a receding galaxy appears red, but this is not the case. It is still seen through the eye's "window" of white light, but the wavelength of the rays that are now shining through that window were beyond its limit when they left the galaxy. To a radio telescope on Earth their frequency (note) has been lowered.

▶ **Radio telescopes** are sensitive to long-wave electromagnetic radiation. This one, the 249 foot (76m) dish in Jodrell Bank, England, came into operation in 1955 as the first large steerable radio telescope in the world.

The Milky Way and beyond

Pulsars and quasars

Pulsars were detected in 1967 as faint, regular pulses of radio signals, so brief and artificial-looking that they were once thought to be artificial messages.

Further work proved that they came from interstellar objects, some of which are spinning more than 100 times per second. The only possible known candidate is a *neutron star*—the collapsed core of a supernova, in which the star's remaining material is compressed into a body that is only a couple of miles across. A pinhead of neutron-star material would weigh as much as a battleship. If our bodies were compressed into the solid, atomic nuclear material they contain, we would be invisible without a microscope.

This was proven when the faint star at the center of the Crab Nebula, the famous supernova remnant (see page 55), was found to be pulsing at a high speed. The intense magnetic field of the star may be responsible for forcing its radiation into a narrow beam like that of a lighthouse.

Quasars

Quasars, or quasi-stellar objects, are the most powerful known energy sources in the universe. They appear to be much smaller than ordinary galaxies (although there is considerable uncertainty about their size), but they emit hundreds of times as much radiation.

One explanation of a quasar is that a massive black hole at the center of a galaxy causes material from the rest of the galaxy to swirl into it at almost the speed of light. This material would radiate energy on the scale observed. However, observations from the Hubble Space Telescope show that some quasars seem to be singular bright objects with no surrounding gas and dust to "fuel" them.

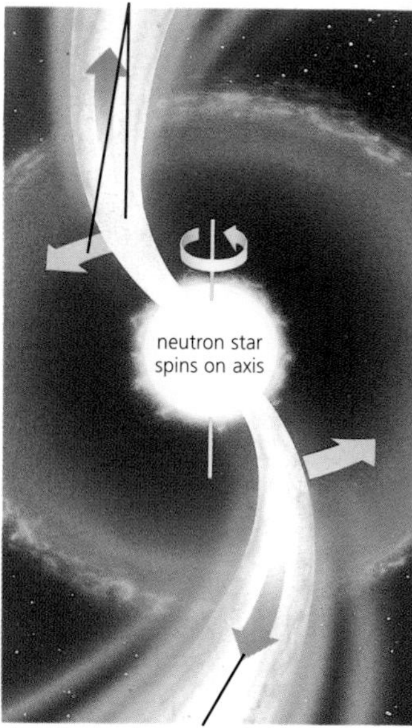

▲ **The fierce radiation** from a spinning neutron star is squirted like water into two opposite narrow jets as its magnetic and gravitational fields intertwine. If Earth lies in the plane of its spin, regular bursts of radiation will be detected.

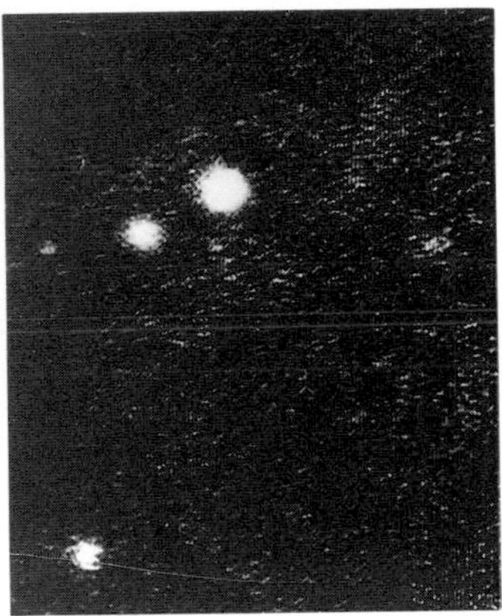

▲ **These two photographs** reveal the pulsar at the center of the Crab Nebula. It is alternately bright (left) and invisible (right) 30 times every second.

Large redshifts

All quasars have very large redshifts, which suggests that they are very far away; we are seeing them as they were billions of years ago, when the universe was younger than it is today. Perhaps they are short-lived objects of the early universe or an early stage of galaxy formation.

Objects such as quasars and pulsars are among the most significant astronomical discoveries of the 1900s. Just as the *Voyager* and *Cassini* probes have made physicists puzzle over the nature of Saturn's rings, so the energy production of quasars and the formation of pulsars have made scientists reexamine what they know about the nature of the physical world.

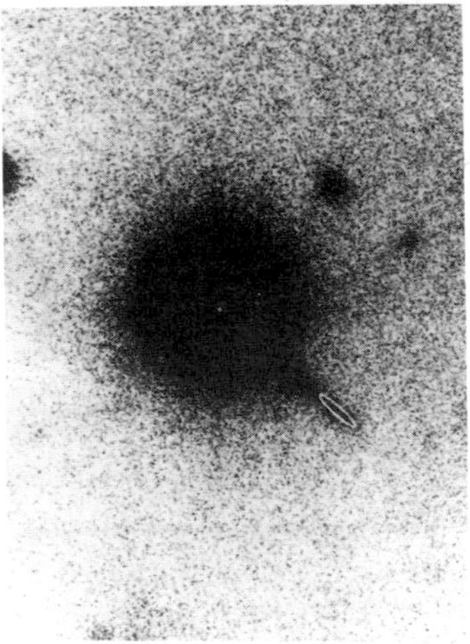

▲ **Quasar 3C 273,** around 600 million light-years away, is one of the closest and brightest known quasars.

Simple astrophotography

Star photographs can be taken using fast film in a 35 millimeter single lens reflex camera. Start by setting the lens on its widest aperture and exposing the film for around 30 seconds. Practice will determine the exact settings and the time that is needed. The photographs here were taken in this way. Digital cameras that allow timed exposures can also be used to achieve similar results.

The Pleiades picture opposite shows how much can be recorded without any special equipment, since most of these stars are difficult to see—or even invisible—with the naked eye. If the shutter is left open for one minute or less, the stars form short trails of light. Longer exposure means longer trails. Tracking the stars with the camera as Earth turns will achieve sharp images. In this case the camera is attached to a motor-driven mounting.

▶ **The Pleiades** in the constellation Taurus, photographed using a stationary camera with a telephoto lens. Earth's rotation has made the stars drift during the exposure.

▲ **A digital camera** is propped up, ready to photograph the stars. Once the exposure time is set, the timer is used to trigger the shutter to avoid jostling the camera.

▼ **The constellation** of Coma Berenices, photographed with a camera that has been guided to stay fixed on the stars.

Astrophotography with a telescope

A camera can be mounted onto a telescope in one of two ways. It can be mounted to the telescope tube in a piggyback fashion, leaving the eyepiece free for observation. Alternatively, it can be mounted in place of the telescope's eyepiece. This way the camera is attached to the telescope so that the image formed by the telescope's objective lens or mirror is focused sharply on the film. This is necessary for close-up pictures. Exposures must be shorter than around half a second, or Earth's rotation will noticeably blur the image. An equatorial telescope with a drive will keep the camera pointed to its target and allow longer exposure times.

Specialist digital cameras, which do not use conventional film, are excellent for capturing images of individual objects. These record on light-sensitive silicon chips—termed CCDs (charge-coupled devices)—that convert light into digital data to produce an image. A few years ago, the CCD system was mostly used by professional astrophotographers. Today it is the favored choice of most amateurs. The CCD system is 10–20 times more sensitive than photographic film, and so exposure times are adjusted accordingly. CCDs are also able to capture images of fainter objects and record greater detail.

Images recorded onto home digital cameras and more specialist CCD systems can be transferred to, and stored on, home computer systems. Software programs, which allow alteration to the brightness and contrast of an image, can then be used to enhance the images. It is also possible to use a video camera or a home computer webcam to record a night sky scene.

Modern cameras allow immediate inspection of images taken. This means that the astronomer can adjust the camera settings and take many images without

◀ **A webcam** attached to an amateur astronomer's telescope produces a live video image of the Moon's surface. Good quality still images of the Moon, planets, and stars can be produced from these video frames.

delay. These can then be stored or rejected immediately. The camera settings depend on a number of factors, such as the type of camera, whether the camera is fixed or driven, and on the local conditions, as well as the choice of subject.

Bright stars, comets, and auroras need exposure times of at least ten seconds; as do the Moon and planets at twilight, when foreground details, such as trees, will show up and the planets will be points of light. Close-up shots of the Moon and the planets need a fraction of a second.

► **This equatorially-mounted** reflecting telescope with a 150 millimeter aperture is suitable for photographs of the Moon and brighter planets. It can also be used as a guide telescope for a 35 millimeter or digital camera.

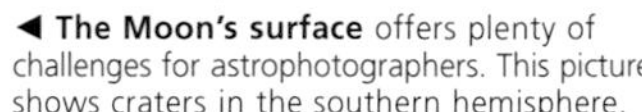

◄ **The Moon's surface** offers plenty of challenges for astrophotographers. This picture shows craters in the southern hemisphere.

▼ **To take successful pictures** of the Sun, a very dense filter is necessary. The photograph below shows the solar disk as it appeared on August 24, 1990.

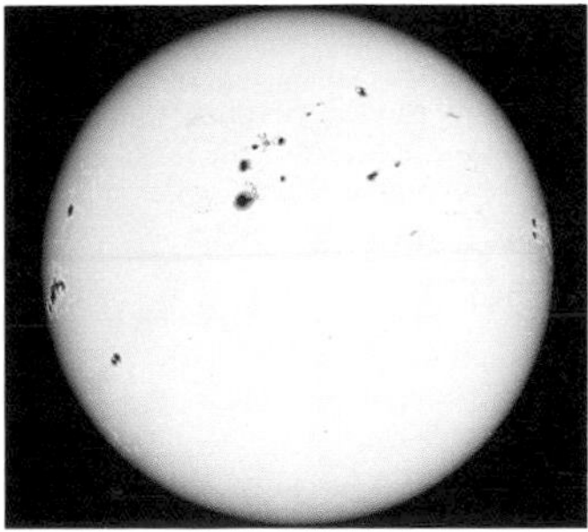

A sky diary

This diary records some of the interesting events in the sky between 2006 and 2009. All times are GMT. More detailed predictions can be found in astronomical yearbooks such as the *Yearbook of Astronomy* (see page 172). Web sites can also tell you what is visible from where you are, once you have entered the date, latitude, and longitude.

2006

Jan. 3 Quadrantid meteor shower at maximum, 16:00.
Jan. 14 Full Moon.
Jan. 27 Saturn at opposition in Cancer.
Feb. 13 Full Moon.
Feb. 24 Mercury at elongation, western sky after sunset.
Mar. 14 Full Moon.
Mar. 25 Venus at elongation, early morning sky before sunrise.
Mar. 29 Total solar eclipse (see page 39).
Apr. 8 Mercury at elongation, eastern sky before sunrise.
Apr. 13 Full Moon.
May 4 Jupiter at opposition in Libra. Eta Aquarids meteor shower at maximum, for southern observers.
May 13 Full Moon.
June 11 Full Moon.
June 20 Mercury at elongation, western sky after sunset.
July 11 Full Moon.
Aug. 7 Mercury at elongation, eastern sky before sunrise.
Aug. 9 Full Moon.
Aug. 10 Neptune at opposition in Capricorn, but still only visible as a tiny disk of light.
Aug. 12 Perseids meteor shower at maximum, 19:00.
Sept. 5 Uranus at opposition in Aquarius, but still only visible as a tiny disk of light.
Sept. 7 Full Moon and partial lunar eclipse (see page 96).
Oct. 7 Full Moon.
Oct. 17 Mercury at elongation, western sky after sunset.
Oct. 20 Orionids meteor shower at maximum.
Nov. 5 Full Moon.
Nov. 8 Transit of Mercury across the Sun's disk at 21:42, lasting 4 hrs. 58 mins. Visible in Pacific Ocean regions only.
Nov. 17 Leonid meteor shower at maximum, 22:00.
Nov. 25 Mercury at elongation, eastern sky before sunrise.
Dec. 5 Full Moon.
Dec. 14 Geminids meteor shower at maximum, 04:00.

2007

Jan. 3 Quadrantid meteor shower at maximum, 22:00. Full Moon.
Feb. 2 Full Moon.
Feb. 7 Mercury at elongation, western sky after sunset.
Feb. 10 Saturn at opposition in Leo.
Mar. 3 Full Moon and total lunar eclipse (see page 96).
Mar. 19 Partial solar eclipse.
Mar. 22 Mercury at elongation, eastern sky before sunrise.
Apr. 2 Full Moon.
May 2 Full Moon.
May 4 Eta Aquarids meteor shower at maximum, for southern observers
June 1 Full Moon
June 2 Mercury at elongation, western sky after sunset.

June 6 Jupiter at opposition in Scorpius.
June 9 Venus at elongation, early evening sky, around sunset.
June 30 Full Moon.
July 20 Mercury at elongation, eastern sky before sunrise.
July 30 Full Moon.
Aug. 13 Perseids meteor shower at maximum, 01:00. Neptune at opposition in Capricorn, but still only visible as a tiny disk of light.
Aug. 28 Full Moon and total lunar eclipse (see page 96).
Sept. 10 Uranus at opposition in Aquarius, but still only visible as a tiny disk of light.
Sept. 11 Partial solar eclipse.
Sept. 26 Full Moon.
Sept. 29 Mercury at greatest elongation, western sky after sunset.
Oct. 20 Orionids meteor shower at maximum.
Oct. 26 Full Moon.
Oct. 28 Venus at elongation, early morning sky before sunrise.
Nov. 8 Mercury at elongation, eastern sky before sunrise.
Nov. 18 Leonid meteor shower at maximum, 04:00.
Nov. 24 Full Moon.
Dec. 14 Geminids meteor shower at maximum, 10:00.
Dec. 24 Full Moon and Mars at opposition in Gemini.

2008
Jan. 4 Quadrantid meteor shower at maximum, 04:00.
Jan. 22 Full Moon and Mercury at elongation; western sky after sunset.
Feb. 21 Full Moon and total lunar eclipse (see page 96).
Feb. 24 Saturn at opposition in Leo.
Mar. 3 Mercury at elongation, eastern sky before sunrise.
Mar. 21 Full Moon.
Apr. 20 Full Moon.
May 4 Eta Aquarids meteor shower at maximum, for southern observers.
May 14 Mercury at elongation, western sky after sunset.
May 20 Full Moon.
June 18 Full Moon.
July 1 Mercury at elongation, eastern sky before sunrise.
July 9 Jupiter at opposition in Sagittarius.
July 18 Full Moon.
Aug. 1 Total solar eclipse (see page 39).
Aug. 12 Perseids meteor shower at maximum, 07:00.
Aug. 15 Neptune at opposition in Capricorn, but still only visible as a tiny disk of light.
Aug. 16 Full Moon and partial lunar eclipse (see page 96).
Sept. 11 Mercury at elongation, western sky after sunset.
Sept. 13 Uranus at opposition in Aquarius, but still only visible as a tiny disk of light.
Sept. 15 Full Moon.
Oct. 14 Full Moon.
Oct. 20 Orionids meteor shower at maximum.
Oct. 22 Mercury at elongation, eastern sky before sunrise.
Nov. 13 Full Moon.
Nov. 17 Leonid meteor shower at maximum, 10:00.
Dec. 12 Full Moon.
Dec. 13 Geminids meteor shower at maximum, 16:00.

A sky diary

2009

Jan. 3 Quadrantid meteor shower at maximum, 10:00.

Jan. 4 Mercury at elongation, western sky after sunset.

Jan. 11 Full Moon.

Jan. 14 Venus at elongation, early evening sky, around sunset.

Feb. 9 Full Moon.

Feb. 13 Mercury at elongation, eastern sky before sunrise.

Mar. 8 Saturn at opposition in Leo.

Mar. 11 Full Moon.

Apr. 9 Full Moon.

Apr. 26 Mercury at elongation, western sky after sunset.

May 4 Eta Aquarids meteor shower at maximum, for southern observers.

May 9 Full Moon.

June 5 Venus at elongation, early morning sky before sunrise.

June 7 Full Moon.

June 13 Mercury at elongation, eastern sky before sunrise.

July 7 Full Moon.

July 22 Total solar eclipse (see page 39).

Aug. 6 Full Moon.

Aug. 12 Perseids meteor shower at maximum, 13:00.

Aug. 14 Jupiter at opposition in Capricorn.

Aug. 17 Neptune at opposition in Aquarius.

Aug. 24 Mercury at elongation, western sky after sunset.

Sept. 4 Full Moon.

Sept. 17 Uranus at opposition in Pisces, but still only visible as a tiny disk of light.

Oct. 4 Full Moon.

Oct. 6 Mercury at elongation, eastern sky before sunrise.

Oct. 20 Orionids meteor shower at maximum.

Nov. 2 Full Moon.

Nov. 17 Leonid meteor shower at maximum, 16:00.

Dec. 2 Full Moon.

Dec. 13 Geminids meteor shower at maximum, 22:00.

Dec. 18 Mercury at elongation, western sky after sunset.

Dec. 31 Full Moon and partial lunar eclipse (see page 96).

Key dates in astronomical history

B.C.

c. 3000 Babylonian astronomical records begin.

c. 1000 Chinese astronomical records begin.

c. 280 Aristarchus suggests that Earth orbits the Sun.

c. 270 Eratosthenes makes an accurate estimate of the size of Earth

c. 130 Hipparchus draws up the first star catalog.

A.D.

c. 140 Ptolemy's Almagest written; his Earth-centered universe is accepted.

903 Star positions measured by Al-Sufi.

1054 Supernova in Taurus recorded by Chinese astronomers.

1433 Ulugh Beigh's star catalog is compiled.

1543 Nicolaus Copernicus proposes a Sun-centered system.

1572 Supernova in Cassiopeia observed by Tycho Brahe.

1600 Johannes Kepler starts analyzing Tycho's planetary observations and derives his three laws of planetary motion (1609–1618).

1608 The refracting telescope is invented by Hans Lippershey.

1609 Galileo and others make the first telescopic observations.

1631 Transit of Mercury across the Sun, predicted by Kepler, is observed by Gassendi.

1638 Holwarda discovers the famous variable star Mira Ceti.

1647 One of the first lunar maps is drawn by Hevelius.

1668 Isaac Newton constructs the first reflecting telescope.

1687 Newton's *Principia*, containing his theory of gravitation, is published.

1705 Edmond Halley predicts that the comet last seen in 1682 will return again in 1758.

1725 The first "modern" star catalog, based on Flamsteed's observations, is published.

1758 John Dollond manufactures the first successful achromatic object-glass. Halley's comet makes its predicted return.

1761 The first transit of Venus across the Sun is observed.

1781 William Herschel discovers the new planet Uranus, and Charles Messier publishes his catalog of star clusters and nebulae.

1801 Giuseppe Piazzi discovers the first asteroid, Ceres.

▼ **Astronomers** in Istanbul Observatory in the Middle Ages. Notice the astronomical instruments they used.

Key dates in astronomical history

1834 Bessel discovers the first white dwarf star, the companion of Sirius.

1838 Friedrich Wilhelm Bessel makes the first interstellar distance measurement—of 61 Cygni.

1840 The first astronomical photograph, of the Moon, is taken by John William Draper.

1843 The sunspot cycle is announced by Samuel Heinrich Schwabe.

1846 Neptune is discovered as a result of predictions by John Couch Adams and Urbain Leverrier.

1859 Gustav Kirchhoff proves that the elements in a hot body imprint characteristic lines in its spectrum.

1863 Secchi makes pioneer observations of the spectra of stars and divides them into "families".

1870–1900 Great developments in astronomical photography and spectrum analysis.

1877 Legendary opposition of Mars, when Schiaparelli announced that he had discovered channels ("canals").

1891 George Ellery Hale invents the spectroheliograph for photographing the Sun at a single wavelength.

1908 The Hertzsprung-Russell diagram introduces the idea of giant and dwarf stars. The first of the "giant" reflecting telescopes, the five-foot (1.5-m) telescope on Mount Wilson, begins work.

1912 The Cepheid period-luminosity law is announced by Henrietta Leavitt.

1920 Redshift is first noticed in distant galaxies.

1923 Edwin Powell Hubble takes the first good measurement of the distance of M31 in Andromeda.

1930 Clyde Tombaugh discovers Pluto.

1930–1960 Many investigations are made into stellar energy production and the evolution of stars.

1937 The first radio waves from space are detected by Grote Reber.

1948 The Mount Palomar 16 foot (5m) reflector is completed.

1955 The Jodrell Bank 249 foot (76m) radio telescope is completed.

1963 The great distances of quasars are established. Background radiation pervading space is discovered.

1967 Pulsars are discovered by Jocelyn Bell and Anthony Hewish. The Moon's independence is assured under the United Nations Treaty on Outer Space.

1987 Supernova observed in the Large Magellanic Cloud.

1992 The first Kuiper Belt Object, 1992 QB1, is discovered.

1994 Comet Shoemaker-Levy 9 crashes into Jupiter.

1995 NASA releases the "Deep Field" images from the Hubble Space Telescope, revealing no less than 1,500 galaxies at various stages of development.

2001 International team discover eleven distant planets. Number of known planets (outside solar system) rises to 63.

Key dates in space exploration

1804 The first high-altitude ascent is made by Gay-Lussac and Biot in a hot air balloon, reaching a height of four miles (7km).
1896 Unmanned balloons, launched by Teisserenc de Bort, analyze the atmosphere at heights of up to nine miles (15km).
1903 Ziolkovsky proposes a rocket-propelled spacecraft.
1919 Goddard publishes a monograph on rocket propulsion.
1923 Oberth's book *The Rocket into Interplanetary Space* is published.
1926 Goddard launches the first liquid-fueled rocket.
1942 Experiments with the V2 rocket at Peenemünde achieve heights of 112 miles (180km).
1949 The first two-stage rocket, the WAC-Corporal, achieves a height of 248 miles (400km).
1950 Cape Canaveral is first used for rocket experiments.
1955 The U.S. announces its intention to launch space satellites.
1957 The world's first satellite, *Sputnik 1*, is launched by the U.S.S.R. on October 4th.
1958 *Explorer 1*, the first satellite launched by the U.S., discovers radiation belts around Earth.
1959 Three lunar probes are launched by the U.S.S.R.: *Luna 3* photographs the farside; *Luna 2* hits the surface.
1961 The first manned orbital flight, by U.S.S.R. astronaut Gagarin in *Vostok*.
1962 The first successful interplanetary probe, *Mariner 2*, sends back information about Venus.
1964 The first close-up pictures of the Moon are obtained by *Ranger 7* (U.S.).
1965 *Mariner 4* (U.S.) passes Mars and transmits pictures and information.
1966 *Venera 3* (U.S.S.R.) lands on Venus—the first spacecraft to reach another planet. *Luna 9* (U.S.S.R.) makes the first soft landing on the Moon, followed by *Surveyor 1* (U.S.). The first of the *Orbiter* mapping lunar satellites is launched (U.S.).
1967 *Venera 4* (U.S.S.R.) soft-lands on Venus and sends back information.
1969 *Mariner 6* and *7* (U.S.) pass Mars and send back pictures and information. *Apollo 11* lands the first men on the Moon (July 20th).
1970 The first automatic lunar probe, *Luna 16* (U.S.S.R.), returns a sample to Earth.
1971 *Mariner 9* (U.S.) orbits Mars. *Salyut 1*, the first-ever space station, is launched by the U.S.S.R.
1972 The last manned mission to the Moon, in *Apollo 17*.
1973 The first flyby of Jupiter by *Pioneer 10*, which becomes the first man-made artifact to escape from the solar system. *Skylab*, an orbiting astronomical laboratory, is launched by the U.S. and visited by three different teams.
1974 *Mariner 10* (U.S.) passes both Venus and Mercury. *Salyut 3* and *4* (U.S.S.R.) link up to form an orbiting observatory. *Pioneer 11* (U.S.) passes Jupiter and heads for Saturn.
1976 The first successful landings on Mars by the two *Viking* craft (U.S.).
1977 *Voyagers 1* and *2* launched toward the outer planets.
1978 *Pioneer Venus* project (U.S.) puts

two craft into orbit around Venus and lands four surface probes.

1979 *Voyagers 1* and *2* (U.S.) pass Jupiter. *Pioneer 11* passes Saturn successfully after a six-year journey.

1980 *Voyager 1* makes a successful flyby of Saturn and heads for outer space.

1981 The first space shuttle, *Columbia* (U.S.), completes two flights. *Voyager 2* passes Saturn.

1982 The U.S.S.R. sends a probe to Venus.

1986 The space shuttle *Challenger* explodes during takeoff. *Voyager 2* sends back photographs of Uranus and its moons. The *Giotto* space probe passes through Halley's Comet. The core module of the Russian Space Station *Mir* is launched.

1989 *Voyager 2* passes Neptune, its last planetary target.

1990 Hubble Space Telescope is launched. *Magellan* probe goes into orbit around Venus, mapping most of the surface of Venus by means of radar; the Cosmic Background Explorer satellite examines the Big Bang background radiation.

1991 The *Galileo* Jupiter probe obtains the first close-up view of an asteroid.

1992 NASA begins the ten-year SETI project to search for extraterrestrial radio transmissions.

1993 Contact is lost with the *Mars Observer* spacecraft just three days before it was due to go into orbit around the planet.

1994 After a shuttle repair mission the Hubble Space Telescope performance is greatly improved.

1995 *Galileo* orbits Jupiter and transmits pictures and data. First rendezvous of a NASA spacecraft with *Mir*.

1997 *Mars Pathfinder* parachutes down to Mars and analyzes Martian rocks for three months. *Cassini* is launched and scheduled to reach Saturn's orbit by 2004. *Mars Global Surveyor* is launched to Mars.

1998 The first part of the International Space Station is launched.

1999 *Stardust* probe is launched to intercept Comet Wild 2 and return sample material by 2006.

2001 Space tourist Denis Tito pays $20 million for an eight-day visit to the ISS. *Mir* falls to Earth: its life is over.

2003 *Mars Express*, Europe's first interplanetary probe, is launched to Mars, where it will image the entire surface of the planet.

2004 Two NASA rovers, *Spirit* and *Opportunity*, explore Mars on opposite sides of the planet. The *Messenger* probe is launched to Mercury. *Cassini* starts its four-year study of Saturn and its rings and moons.

► **An American astronaut** leans out into space, while anchored to a remote manipulator system (RMS).

Key dates in space exploration

Glossary

HOW THE SUN SHINES

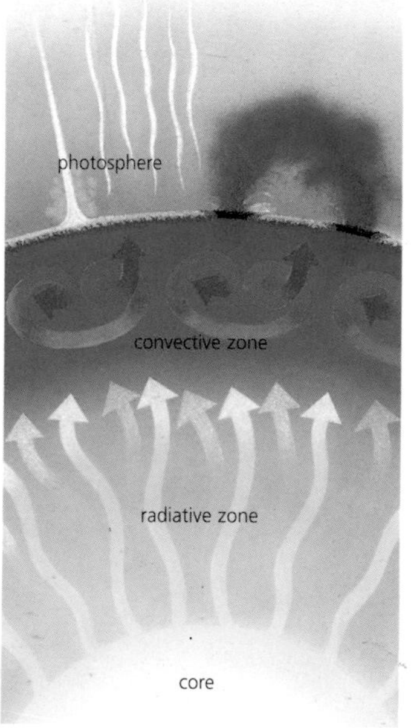

Not all these words are used in the book, but they are useful terms, and they could be ones that you come across as an amateur astronomer.

absorption spectrum Spectrum crossed by dark lines due to light absorbed by intervening cool gas.

achromatic lens Used in a refracting telescope to give a color-free image. A non-achromatic lens produces false color fringes around objects in the sky.

aerolite A meteorite mostly consisting of stony material.

airglow Faint auroral luminosity of the night sky.

albedo The ratio of light reflected to light received.

altitude The height of an object above the horizon, measured in degrees (°).

aphelion The point on the orbit of a planetary body that is farthest from the Sun.

apogee The point on the orbit of a satellite that is farthest from the planet.

Astronomical Unit (AU) The mean distance of Earth from the Sun (92,750,679 miles).

binary star A pair of stars orbiting around each other.

chromosphere The inner atmosphere of the Sun.

coma The head of a comet.

comes The faint companion of a double star.

conjunction Occurs when a planet, Earth, and the Sun are in line. In the case of Mercury and Venus, which can come between Earth and the Sun, they are said to be at inferior conjunction on the near side of the Sun and at superior conjunction on the far side.

corona The Sun's outer atmosphere.

declination A coordinate for finding objects in the sky. The equivalent of latitude on Earth.

dichotomy The half-phase of the Moon or a planet.

Doppler shift The change of wavelength of sound or light waves due to motion between the source and the observer.

eccentricity The word used to describe the difference between an ellipse and a circle. A very eccentric ellipse is a long, thin loop.

ecliptic The path followed by the Sun over the course of one year.

ellipse The oval path traced by the planets and many comets.

elongation The angle of Mercury or Venus from the Sun at any given time.

emission spectrum Spectrum of bright lines, caused by luminous gas.

eyepiece The lens or group of lenses in a telescope against which the eye is placed. It magnifies the image made by the object's glass or mirror.

fireball A meteor brighter than the planet Venus. ▲

focal length The distance between a lens or mirror and the image it forms of a remote object.

Fraunhöfer lines The absorption lines in the solar spectrum.

galaxy A star system. "The galaxy" refers to the galaxy to which our Sun belongs. ▼

TYPES OF GALAXIES

irregular galaxies

elliptical galaxies

ordinary spiral galaxies

barred spiral galaxies

Glossary

gegenschein A very faint permanent glow in the sky opposite the Sun.
granulation The fine, mottled texture of the Sun's surface.
hour angle The time in sidereal hours between a celestial object's present position and its meridian transit.
ionosphere The upper layer of Earth's atmosphere (above around 43 miles) where most atoms have either lost or gained electrons and are therefore ionized.
light-year Distance traveled by light in one year (5,865,634,000,000 miles).
limb The edge of the Sun, Moon, or a planet as it is seen in the sky.
luminosity A measure of light produced by a star.
lunation The interval from one new Moon to the next.
magnitude A scale that measures the brightness of a star.
magnetosphere The shell of charged particles held around Earth by its magnetic field.
meridian An imaginary line crossing the sky and passing through the zenith and the Northern and Southern celestial poles.
midnight Sun The presence of the Sun above the horizon at midnight in high latitudes, when its distance from the celestial pole is less than the pole's altitude.
node The point at which the orbit of the Moon or a planet crosses the plane of Earth's orbit (ecliptic).
occultation The covering of a celestial body by the Moon or a planet.
opposition The instant when a planet is opposite the Sun in the sky.
parallax The slight shift in the position of a nearby star when viewed from opposite sides of Earth's orbit.
periastron The closest approach of two stars in a binary system as seen from Earth.
perigee The point on the orbit of a satellite that is closest to the planet.
perihelion The point on the orbit of a planetary body that is closest to the Sun.
perturbation The departure of a body from its true course due to the gravitational pull of another body.
photosphere The Sun's visible surface.
prominence Eruptions of gas from the surface of the Sun. ▼

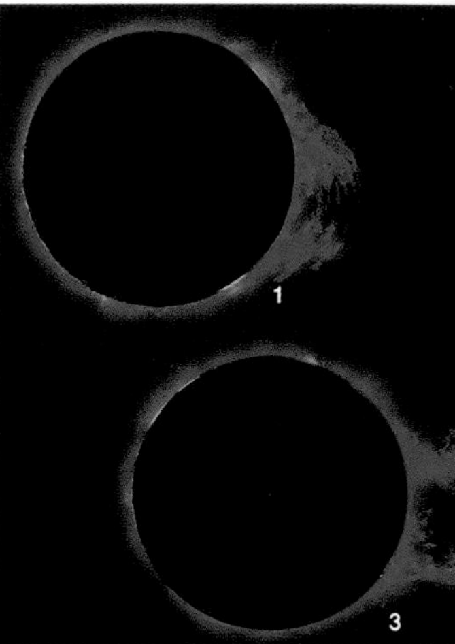

▲ **Four stages** in the eruption and decay of a huge solar prominence, recorded by a space-borne telescope over a period of two days.

proper motion Drift of a star across the celestial sphere due to its own motion.
radial velocity Motion of a star or galaxy toward or away from the observer.
redshift The way in which a star's color reddens when it moves rapidly away from the observer. An approaching object becomes bluer, showing blueshift.

retrograde motion The motion opposite to that which is followed by the planets in their orbits (clockwise as seen from the north).

saros The interval of 18 years and 103 days, after which the Sun, Moon, and Earth are in almost exactly the same relative position, and eclipses will recur.

sidereal day The time taken by Earth to rotate once, as measured by a star: 23 hours, 56 minutes, and 4 seconds long.

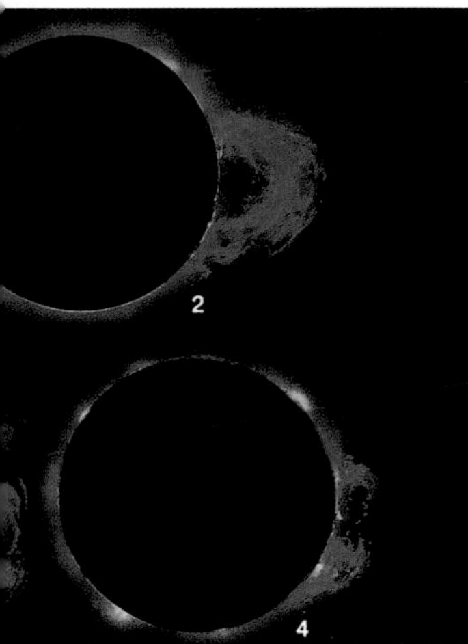

siderite A meteorite mostly consisting of iron.

solar day The time taken by Earth to rotate once, as measured by the Sun: 24 hours.

solar wind The continuous outflow of atomic particles from the Sun.

spectroheliograph An instrument for photographing the Sun in the light emitted by a single element.

stratosphere The layer of calm, cold air lying between 9–25 miles above Earth's surface. ▼

tektites Small, glassy bodies, probably caused by material thrown up when meteorites hit Earth long ago.

transit The passage of a smaller body across the disk of a larger one.

troposphere The lower region of Earth's atmosphere, extending to a height of around nine miles. ▼

wavelength The distance between pulses of radiation.

Wolf-Rayet stars Very hot stars with luminous atmospheres.

zenithal hourly rate (ZHR) The number of meteors per hour that would be seen if the radiant were at the zenith.

zodiacal band An excessively faint band of light extending around the ecliptic caused by interplanetary particles reflecting sunlight.

▼ **The troposphere** contains most of Earth's atmosphere, but traces of air are still found several hundred miles above the surface.

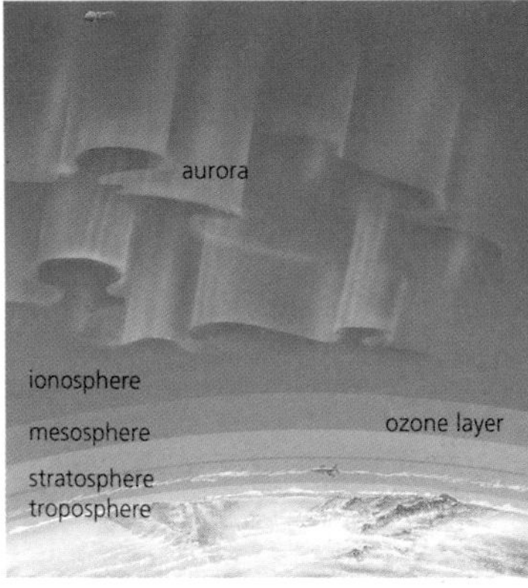

Societies and useful books

If you want to find out more about astronomy, the best way is to join a local group. Societies are always on the lookout for new members, particularly for enthusiasts who want to learn.

You will have the chance of looking through powerful telescopes, of borrowing books from the library (most societies have one), and of getting advice.

This is the most important benefit of all: you will probably find someone who has done astrophotography, someone else who has observed variable stars, and more . . . and you will learn much more by asking them questions than you will from books alone.

Ask at your local library or community center if there is a society in your area.

Astronomical Societies
www.cv.nrao.edu/fits/www/yp_society.html

Astronomical League
The world's largest federation of amateur astronomers. With quick links, observing clubs, updated NASA information, and astronomy events.
www.astroleague.org

Observing clubs through the Astronomical League
www.astroleague.org/observing.html

Books to read
The following books contain plenty of useful information for practical amateurs:

Yearbooks and atlases
Yearbook of Astronomy
edited by Patrick Moore
(Macmillan, annually).

Norton's Star Atlas and Reference Handbook
(Prentice Hall, 2003) is the best star atlas.

Guidebooks
Guide to the Night Sky
by Patrick Moore (Philip, 2005).

The Urban Astronomer
by Gregory Matloff (Wiley, 1991).

Exploring the Night Sky with Binoculars
by Patrick Moore
(Cambridge University Press, 2000).

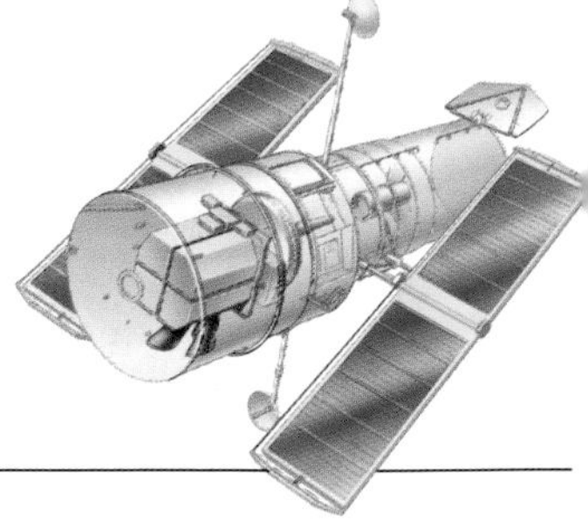

► **The Hubble Space Telescope**, launched in 1990, orbits Earth's surface and uses a mirror that is eight feet (2.4m) across.

Index

Acknowledgments

Photographs: Page 8 Kitt Peak Observatory; 11 Galaxy Picture Library; 15 Long & Wood; 20 Galaxy Picture Library; 77 Galaxy Picture Library; 79 Y. Hirose/Galaxy; 87 Californian Institute of Technology; 94 Galaxy Picture Library; 97 Galaxy Picture Library; 99 Galaxy Picture Library; 101 Galaxy Picture Library; 113 Jet Propulsion Laboratory; 118 New Mexico State University; 125 NASA; 127 Jet Propulsion Laboratory; 130 Jet Propulsion Laboratory; 131 Jet Propulsion Laboratory; 132 Galaxy Picture Library; 147 Jet Propulsion Laboratory; 155 Royal Astronomical Society; 156 Robin Scagell/Galaxy; 157 Galaxy Picture Library; 158 Robin Scagell/Galaxy; 159 Galaxy Picture Library; 163 & 164 NASA.

All other photographs: Science Photo Library.